W9-BAC-668

THE SHOOTING SCRIPT™

THE ICE STORM

THE ICE STORM

SCREENPLAY, INTRODUCTION, AND NOTES BY

JAMES SCHAMUS

BASED ON THE NOVEL BY RICK MOODY

PREFACE BY

ANG LEE

A Newmarket Shooting Script™ Series Book

NEWMARKET PRESS • NEW YORK

Compilation and design copyright © 1997 by Newmarket Press. All rights reserved.
Trademark and © 1997 Twentieth Century Fox Film Corporation. All rights reserved.
Preface by Ang Lee copyright © 1997 by Ang Lee. All rights reserved.
Introduction by James Schamus copyright © 1997 by James Schamus. All rights reserved.
Screenplay, poster design, and unit photography copyright © 1997 by Fox Searchlight Pictures, Inc. All rights reserved.
All photographs by Barry Wetcher and Adger W. Cowans.

This book published simultaneously in the United States of America and in Canada.

All rights reserved. This book may not be reproduced, in whole or in part,
in any form, without written permission. Inquiries should be addressed to:
Permissions Department, Newmarket Press, 18 East 48th Street, New York, NY 10017.

First Edition

97 98 99   10 9 8 7 6 5 4 3 2 1

Library of Congress Cataloging-in-Publication Data
Schamus, James.
The ice storm : the shooting script / by James Schamus.
    p.   cm. — (A Newmarket shooting script series book)
    Adaptation of: The ice storm / Rick Moody.
        ISBN 1-55704-309-4
    I. Ice storm (Motion picture) II. Moody, Rick. Ice storm.
        III. Title. IV. Series.
        PN1997.I226   1996
791.43'72—DC20   96-27208
                                                           CIP

Quantity Purchases
Companies, professional groups, clubs, and other organizations may qualify for
special terms when ordering quantities of this title. For information, write to Special Sales,
Newmarket Press, 18 East 48th Street, New York, NY 10017, or call (212) 832-3575.

Book design by Tania Garcia.
Manufactured in the United States of America.

OTHER NEWMARKET SHOOTING SCRIPTS™ INCLUDE

U-Turn: The Shooting Script
Swept from the Sea: The Shooting Script
The People vs. Larry Flynt: The Shooting Script
Dead Man Walking: The Shooting Script

The Birdcage: The Shooting Script
The Shawshank Redemption: The Shooting Script
A Midwinter's Tale: The Shooting Script
The Age of Innocence: The Shooting Script

OTHER NEWMARKET MOVIEBOOKS INCLUDE

The Seven Years in Tibet Screenplay and Story Behind the Film
Men in Black: The Script and the Story Behind the Film
The Age of Innocence: A Portrait of the Film Based on the Novel by Edith Wharton
The Sense and Sensibility Screenplay & Diaries
Showgirls: Portrait of a Film
Panther: A Pictorial History of the Black Panthers and the Story Behind the Film
Mary Shelley's Frankenstein: The Classic Tale of Terror Reborn on Film
Bram Stoker's Dracula: The Film and the Legend

Dances with Wolves: The Illustrated Story of the Epic Film
Far and Away: The Illustrated Story of a Journey from Ireland to America in the 1890s
Gandhi: A Pictorial Biography
The Inner Circle: An Inside View of Soviet Life Under Stalin
City of Joy: The Illustrated Story of the Film
Neil Simon's Lost in Yonkers: The Illustrated Screenplay of the Film
Last Action Hero: The Official Moviebook
Rapa Nui: The Easter Island Legend on Film
Wyatt Earp: The Film and the Filmmakers
Wyatt Earp's West: Images and Words

CONTENTS

For their help with the preparation of this volume, the author would like to thank Jeff Knapp, Nancy Kricorian, Kelly Miller, and Nevette Previd.

PREFACE

BY ANG LEE

When I think of *The Ice Storm,* I think first of water and rain, of how it falls everywhere, seeps into everything, forms underground rivers, and helps to shape a landscape. And also, when calm, of how it forms a reflective surface, like glass, in which the world reappears. Then, as the temperature drops, what was only water freezes. Its structure can crush concrete and push iron away, it is so strong. Its pattern overthrows everything.

This is the structure I have hoped to create in my movie, *The Ice Storm.* Whatever the surface patterns you might see reflected there, the customs and morals, and hopes, and loves of the characters are infused, and overturned, and reestablished by the force of nature that the storm represents.

When I read Rick Moody's novel, I knew immediately that I wanted to make it into a film. For me, such a revelation comes through small details and particular moments. In this case, it was the moment at the end of the novel when Paul is joined at the train station by his family. The power of the novel is to make of this moment no more and no less than what it is. It is an image that has the force of memory, and for that reason an image that has more meaning than any theme or story or even emotion can give it.

I also thought a great deal about the sounds that an ice storm would make, not just the howling of the wind and rain, but the sounds that come afterwards, as the entire world becomes covered in transparent crackling glass. It was these elemental feelings that brought me to *The Ice Storm.* From there, through the pre-production process, I began to see how important the social and historical side of the book was, and how Rick Moody, through the individual stories he told, was exploring the greatest themes of American history and experience. My producers and I often joked that 1973 was America's most "embarrassing" year, with Nixon, polyester, the admitting of defeat in Vietnam, stagflation, the energy crisis. But embarrassment can be a profound and enlightening experience. In researching for the film, my production team and I read many of the novels and self-help books from the period, and watched many movies made in the early seventies. Rather than approach the period as one of "kitsch," this process led us to a tremendous respect and humility. It turned out that there were many truths buried inside the pop psychology and sometimes painfully naive self-help philosophies of the day, and that we two decades later have much to learn from this "embarrassing" past.

INTRODUCTION

BY JAMES SCHAMUS

CENSORING *THE ICE STORM*

Rick Moody's 1994 novel *The Ice Storm* plays a neat trick, and a decidedly uncinematic one. Told in a knowing, omniscient voice, the book reveals in its final page that that voice is in fact owned by one of the ensemble of the novel's characters. That revelation is a moment of great power, for it is a turn that makes of the novel's story an act of remembering, a search for meaning and truth by someone who, in the most fundamental way, *survived*. Moody has until that final moment played brilliantly on the literary and emotional tension that comes from the contrast between the third-person telling of the story and the particular character of the voice of that telling. It's an old and fruitful tension: To the extent a narrator has a character, a voice, a personality, how could that narrator be omniscient, all-knowing? Wouldn't he or she be a simple, limited mortal like the rest of us?

To write, especially from memory, and especially into fiction, is to take our first-person limitations and test them against the rigors of a third-person imagination. Such an endeavor may be mere hubristic folly, but it is often just this folly that enables us to widen the scope of our recognitions.

Narrative film, in most of its current incarnations, has a hard time engaging in this fruitful tension. Our storytelling conventions, especially in Hollywood, make the cinema an emphatically third-person activity, as if the simple mechanics of film technology cowed us into shying away from more first-person approaches. Hollywood has from time to time toyed with first-person narration, as in Robert Montgomery's *Lady in the Lake,* where a combination of voice-over and continuous point-of-view shots attempted the job. But there's usually something tiresome about the effects, and such experiments have succeeded mainly in the great avant-garde personal cinemas (and videos—another topic) of filmmakers like Chris Marker, Michael Wallin, Jonas Mekas, and Su Friedrich.

So in adapting the novel for the screen, we were faced with an immediate technical problem: Could we find some kind of filmic equivalent to the novel's powerful literary devices, one that retained at least some hint of the book's emotional and philosophical grandeur? The answer, unsurprisingly, was no.

Instead, we came up with a series of *ad hoc* approaches that we hope, in total, might do the trick. While the novel unfolds during a single twenty-four-hour period, filling in its back story through running commentary, we created an entire first hour of the film from hints dropped by Moody in that commentary, picking up where the novel begins about halfway through the script. We turned voice into action.

More important, the novel frequently allows its characters to act in hilariously ill-advised ways while still retaining the reader's sympathies. But reading, for example, about Paul's horrifically endearing bout of masturbation at Libbets's apartment is one thing—seeing it would have been something else altogether, in particular if that image were stripped of the help the book's narrator gives us in appreciating the moment in all its pathos and humor. Without the defining echo of the book's implied first person, the scene (and many others like it) would read as pruriently desperate, especially if thrown explicitly against the screen.

So we found ourselves censoring—censoring not so much the images and scenes from the book but the very voice that had originally made sense of them. It is in such acts of silencing that, I suppose, most adaptations define themselves. I can only hope that the final result is itself a compelling enough testament to the respect and admiration that started the whole process off in the first place.

MAKING *THE ICE STORM*

The shooting script published here is the draft we went into pre-production with. The finished film is quite a different animal. Freak snow storms, equipment failures, sick actors, lack of time, and the hundreds of other contingencies that make up a film shoot all intervened to cause the usual assortment of changes. Some of the scenes you'll read were never shot (the therapy scenes—an homage to late sixties' and seventies' films like Paul Mazursky's wonderful *Bob & Carol & Ted & Alice*—were cut simply because we ran over-time and decided they were expendable); other scenes got left on the editing room floor, mainly because Ang's first cut of the film was over two and a half hours long and something had to go. A shooting script, at the end of the day, is simply a series of suggestions to the director, cast, and crew about how to use their time and spend the film's budget. The more coherent those sugges-tions, the better. Best of all is when they serve merely as a pretext and foundation for the collective experience of surprise and discovery that makes filmmaking so much fun—and films so different from their scripts.

Shooting commenced on a chilly morning in April 1996, in Waveny Park, New Canaan. As is now usual with Ang Lee's films, the day began with a "Big Luck" ceremony, at which crew, cast, and friends all gather and bow, incense in hand, to the four corners of the earth. Ang stands before the group, and, after a moment's silence and the final bow, he bangs a gong and invites the crowd to share some of the ceremonial feast laid out on a table before them. It's a ceremony both mildly ridiculous and surprisingly effective in its communal impact. On *The Wedding Banquet,* the young nonunion crew crowded the sidewalk across the street from New York's City Hall on a busy Monday morning, as politicians and bureaucrats pushed by us; on *Sense and Sensibility,* the grizzled English crew stood before the imposing Saltram House manor in Devon, joined by Emma Thompson and Kate Winslet in their silk Empire dresses and hair curlers. *The Ice Storm* assembly, with our cast in their garish seventies' outfits, was witnessed by a few of New Canaan's wealthy denizens and their dogs who happened to be passing by on their morning walks.

Whatever Big Luck the ceremony brought was not in the weather depart-ment. By midday the sky had turned from gray to icy white, and soon after our first shot, of Kevin Kline walking through the woods, the snow began to fall. As everyone who worked on the film soon learned, snow storms and ice storms are two very different things—ice storms are in fact rain storms during which the temperature falls below freezing—but we decided to keep shooting anyway, and you can see the snow falling as Kevin Kline lifts Christina Ricci on their walk home from the Carvers'. (We shot a swiftly written newscast explaining the day's "light snowfall turning to heavy rains" later on in the shoot.)

As we settled into New Canaan for our first month of shooting, it quickly became apparent that many of the local townspeople were not overjoyed by our presence. The reasons were both specific and general. On the general side, one supposes that the reason people spend as much as they do to live in wealthy hamlets like New Canaan is precisely so they can avoid things like film crews in their midst. Traffic disruptions, crowds of onlookers, and blocks of parked trucks, trailers, and minivans didn't blend easily with the quaint storefronts and Colonial-style mansions. As for specifics, many of the townspeople had read Rick Moody's novel, and a few of them made vocal and very public note of its frank depiction of the sexual revolution's impact on the community circa 1973. Rick had grown up in New Canaan, so there was a particular *roman à clef* intensity to the gossip surrounding the book's contents. The result was a stampede of sales of the book at local bookstores and scores of recalls of the copies remaining in the public library.

As one could imagine, initial local press was at first suspicious. But, thankfully, as the weeks unfolded, the tide turned, and the community began to accept our temporary presence. A copy of the script was deposited on reserve at the library for anyone interested in reading it, and a host of letters to the editor of the *Advertizer* came to the defense of our mores and our shooting habits. Hundreds of people turned out on the weekends during the unseasonably hot spring days as we shot the closing scene of the film at the New Canaan train station, where they witnessed our art department transforming the center of town into a sparkling winter wonderland under the eighty-five-degree heat of the blazing sun.

With the weather alternating between heat waves and torrential downpours, the first half of the shoot was transformed into a frantic race against the first appearance of the leaves and buds of May. Since the action of the film supposedly takes place during Thanksgiving, we were constantly tilting the camera away from the riotous bursts of forsythia that seemed to be constantly dogging us. Careful observers of the film will find the odd patch of deciduous green, but overall Ang and cinematographer Fred Elmes, with the help of a dedicated greens department, were able to keep the color tones of the film limited to a muted, fall-like palette.

The final days of the film were spent at the Harlem Armory in New York, where, in the cavernous expanse of its city-block-wide hall, vaulted by a tin roof, we built the Halford key party set and the Carver house basement. Sharing late night meals of fried chicken and collard greens from Sylvia's Restaurant while taking a break from the "Nixon mask" scene could hardly have underscored more the disjunctions between the happy realities of film production and the illusions eventually projected on the film screen.

Over time, film crews become something like extended families, and on *Ice Storm* there were the usual pranks (anyone caught dozing on set was mercilessly Polaroided, usually after the prop department had placed a few beer and vodka bottles around the unsuspecting sleeper). But even more, there was a sense of connection to many of the specific scenes and events in the film. When developing the script, Ang would often ask about the realism of various parts of the action, such as the shoplifting scenes: Would a privileged American girl really do that? Our answer: Ask just about any woman on the crew when we get there. The bong in Paul's dorm room elicited more than a few knowing nods from many of our straightlaced, settled-down family men on set as did the reel-to-reel tape players and bean bag chairs.

But it wasn't *nostalgia* people were feeling. More often than not, a simple sighting of Elijah Wood's and Adam Hann-Byrd's two-tone bell bottoms would sober up even the most rose-tinted observer. The seventies, except for the people *born* during them (many of whom appear actually to be *enthused* by polyester in the current fashion season), tend not to elicit much allegiance from the people who lived through them. Rather, there's a wistful and communally shared sense of relief at having made it safely past the era and, for many people, a sense of genuine surprise that, in fact, many of the songs, books, fashions, and movies of the period are actually *worth* remembering.

Being on a film crew means being surrounded, day in and day out, with the artifacts of the culture and time you are depicting, and there's something about that physical proximity to the material culture of another world that can be very unnerving. As we continued to live in and explore the world of the seventies we were so painstakingly re-creating, we would again and again witness fellow crew members whose first instinct on encountering some long-forgotten shred of cultural detritus (a song, a car, a Marimekko curtain) was to recoil and then, after a thoughtful pause, to reflect and to remember. The Carver rec room seemed, in particular, to provide a mildly therapeutic space, a kind of architectural encounter room, where those who had passed their adolescences in seventies-style angst could receive a few hurried moments of posttraumatic recollection between camera setups.

I always hope that some of that sense of collective energy can be passed directly from the crew onto the screen, and that the script doesn't get too much in the way.

<u>The Ice Storm</u>

Screenplay by
James Schamus

Based on the novel by Rick Moody

Flashforward:

EXT. TRAIN. DARKNESS BEFORE DAWN.   1

Suburban Connecticut, outside of New York City, 1973. The still
after a terrible storm. Trees dripping, their branches torn;
the air warming in the cool blue light just before dawn. The
train lies dark and motionless; a few flashing yellow emergency
lights in front; a work crew removes debris from the track.

INT. TRAIN. PRE-DAWN.   2

Various passengers, huddled uncomfortably, cold, asleep.

On Paul Hood, 15-and-a-half, stoner-preppie look, hunched up in
his seat under the faint emergency exit light. He reads his
<u>Fantastic Four</u> comic book by the pale light of the emergency
exit sign.

Suddenly, the lights begin to flicker on and the hum of the
train's engines returns.

The conductor enters the car, blasting forth in his classic
nasal voice.

                    CONDUCTOR
          Good morning ladies and gentle-
          men--

He sounds like a baseball announcer.

                    PASSENGERS
               (mumbling, ad lib)
          What ladies?

                    CONDUCTOR
          -- this train originating at New
          York's Grand Central Station is
          back in service -- next stop will
          be New Canaan, Connecticut. New
          Canaan, Connecticut, next stop!

He moves on to the next car.

The train begins to move.

Paul rubs his elbow against the window and looks out into the
still-dark early morning.

He looks back down at his comic book.

                              (CONTINUED)

CONTINUED: 2

On the comic book: Reed Richards (also known as Stretch) has zapped his young son with a cosmic ray gun to neutralize the destructive energy that Annihilus has implanted in him.

The Thing, Medusa, Flame, and Richards' wife Sue Storm look on, stunned.

> "THEN YOU'VE TURNED HIM INTO A
> VEGETABLE. YOUR OWN SON." "DON'T
> YOU SEE, SUE? HE WAS TOO
> POWERFUL...IF HIS ENERGY HAD
> CONTINUED TO BUILD, HE WOULD HAVE
> DESTROYED THE WORLD!"

Paul looks up again, thinking.

> PAUL
> (voice over)
> In issue number 141 of The
> Fantastic Four, published in
> November 1973, Reed Richards has
> to use his anti-matter weapon on
> his own son, who Annihilus has
> turned into a human atom bomb.
> The problem is that the cosmic
> rays that infused Richards and the
> rest of the Fantastic Four on
> their aborted moon mission have
> made young Franklin a volatile
> mixture of matter and anti-matter.

EXT. TRAIN BRIDGE. PRE-DAWN. 3

The train moves slowly through a suburban, semi-forested landscape.

> PAUL
> (v.o. cont'd)
> And that's what it is to come from
> a family, if you analyze it
> closely. Your family is kind of
> like your own personal negative
> matter. And that's what dying is
> -- dying is when your family takes
> you back, thus throwing you into
> negative space....

INT. TRAIN. CONT'D.   4

On Paul, as the sun breaks over the horizon. His face glows
warmly in the yellow light. He looks down idly at the comic
book.

                    PAUL
                  (v.o. cont'd)
          So it's a paradox -- the closer
          you're drawn back in, the further
          into the void you go. And that's
          what happened the morning of the
          ice storm -- the morning death
          became a member of my family...

EXT. CONRAIL STATION. EARLY MORNING.   5

The train slowly pulls in.

The train doors open, and Paul, weary from the long night,
emerges. He sees his family gathered at the other end of the
platform -- Ben, 40, a bit worse for wear but still retaining
traces of his boyish looks; Elena, 37, distant and elegant even
in her oversized sweater; and Wendy, 14, a sullen suburban
Lolita.

He pauses, regarding them.

They stand, silent, even dignified, awaiting him.

END FLASHFORWARD:
                                        CUT TO:

INT. HOOD HOUSE. LIVING ROOM. DAY.   6

A suburban Connecticut Colonial -- a mixture of a few not-so-
old-money touches and some seventies modular design.

Ben and Elena are mid-argument while she maniacally tidies the
living room.

                    BEN
          You're not saying you want a
          divorce?

                    ELENA
          I'm saying that that's what *you're*
          not saying.

                              (CONTINUED)

CONTINUED:

> BEN
>
> But all I'm saying is that I don't
> want to get dragged to any more of
> those kooky group therapy things
> --

> ELENA
>
> Sure. That's what you say you're
> saying. But what are you *really*
> saying?

> BEN
>
> Well, what do you want me to say?

She continues to clean.

> BEN
>
> All right, look. If it's that
> important to you, let's give it
> one more shot.

> ELENA
>
> You don't really mean it.

> BEN
>
> Well at least I said it.

INT. THERAPIST'S OFFICE. EVENING.

A woman sobs hysterically as a few other couples, Ben and Elena
among them, sit around in a circle. No one moves. Ben is
sublimely uncomfortable.

> DR. PASMIER
> (unctuous)
> Garth, I think what Sue is saying
> here is that she feels oppressed
> by always feeling the need for
> your approval.

> GARTH
>
> No she's not -- she's saying I'm a
> piece of shit.

> DR. PASMIER
>
> Garth --

> GARTH
>
> Just ask her --

                                                        (CONTINUED)

CONTINUED: 7

                         SUE
                    (screaming)
               You piece of shit!

                         GARTH
               I told you so!

Ben just rolls his eyes.

                                        JUMP CUT TO:

INT. THERAPIST'S OFFICE. LATER.   8

Garth and Sue are hugging, crying, and slobbering all over each
other, as the other members of the group gather round them in an
awkward group hug. Dr. Pasmier strokes Garth's hair soothingly.

Ben half participates from the edge of the circle. Elena
glances self-consciously at her husband as she, too, half-
heartedly participates.

                                        JUMP CUT TO:

INT. THERAPIST'S OFFICE. LATER.   9

All seated and calm again.

                         BEN
               So that's what we're evolving into
               -- we're really -- best friends --
               I think. Elena? Right? I think
               we're better friends now than
               we've ever been.

                         MARTY
               In other words you've stopped
               having sex.

                         BEN
               Now wait a sec here Marty --

                         SUE
               We don't have any secrets here,
               Ben. We're here to help each
               other and ourselves -- it's OK not
               to feel OK, because we know you
               really are OK, and --

EXT. PARKING LOT. NIGHT.   10

Ben and Elena walk to the car. He opens her door and walks
around to the driver's side to let himself in.

INT. CAR. NIGHT.   11

Silently, he starts the car and they pull out.

EXT. ST. PETER'S SCHOOL. MORNING.   12

To establish. A typical New England prep school.

INT. ST. PETER'S CLASSROOM. DAY.   13

An English class in progress.

Paul Hood sits blankly, hardly listening, until he hears the
teacher call out.

                    TEACHER
          Who would like to -- Libbets?

Libbets, 15, too earnest and too cute, responds.

                    LIBBETS
          What Dostoevsky is saying here is
          that to be a Christian is to
          choose, because you have to choose
          of your own choice, but since you
          can't choose to be good because
          that would be too rational you
          have to choose to be bad -- it's
          existential.

                    TEACHER
          Thank you Libbets, that's a very
          compelling summary, but --

Paul looks at her, smitten. Marge, Paul's friend, notices his
look.

INT. ST. PETER'S HALLWAY. DAY.   14

As class lets out, Paul accosts Libbets.

                                        (CONTINUED)

CONTINUED: 14

                         PAUL
          Um, Libbets. Hey, Dostoevsky, I'm
          also really a fan, and what you
          were saying, you know, have you
          ever read *The Idiot*?

                         LIBBETS
          The Idiot?

                         PAUL
          If you liked *Notes from
          Underground*, you'll love *The
          Idiot*.

                         LIBBETS
               (turning to go)
          Great, thanks for the tip.

                         PAUL
               (after her)
          The Idiot.

INT. ST. PETER'S HALLWAY. DAY.   15

Paul walks with Marge.

                         PAUL
          I'm in love with Libbets Casey.

                         MARGE
          Yeah, well, you've been in love
          with like every other girl here, I
          was wondering when you'd get
          around to Libbets.

                         PAUL
          It's beyond mere physical
          attraction.

                         MARGE
          That's good, because I don't think
          Libbets is capable of the sex act.

                         PAUL
          Truly? Do speak.

                         MARGE
          My diagnosis -- messed in the
          head.
                              (more)

CONTINUED: 15

> MARGE (Cont'd)
> A poor little rich girl -- I mean
> check out the jeans and fur look.
> And lend your ears to this
> brutality. Like her mom and step-
> dad and her step-sisters are going
> to Switzerland to ski over
> Thanksgiving break -- and like
> they didn't invite her!

> PAUL
> How do you know this shit?

> MARGE
> They did it last year too. It's
> like traditional or something.
> They've got this humongoid Park
> Ave. apartment and she just holes
> up there with a wad of cash.
>   (beat)
> Aren't the hugely wealthy sad?

> PAUL
>   (pause)
> You think Francis is going to beat
> me to the punch here?

> MARGE
> Since he sleeps with every girl
> you ever show an interest in, why
> don't you just keep your Libbets
> fixation a secret from him?

> PAUL
>   (beat)
> I think I already told him about
> it.

> MARGE
> Good thinking, Paul.

INT. DORM ROOM. EVENING.   16

Paul enters the room as his roommate, Francis Davenport IV, a
dissolute son of money, is finishing preparing a four-foot-high
bong.

> PAUL
> I hope you changed the water in
> that bong from last night.

                                                        (CONTINUED)

CONTINUED: 16

> FRANCIS
> (finishing a hit)
> The water, as you call it, is a
> special mixture of amaretto and
> Ben&Ben blended for just the exact
> chemical interaction with the last
> of our precious Thai stick.

Paul reluctantly walks over and takes a hit. He coughs, spewing
uninhaled smoke.

> FRANCIS
> Waste not Master Hood -- that was
> $20 for the bag.

> PAUL
> (gathering books,
> papers, almost talking
> to himself)
> I've been thinking, Francis, you
> know, you are one drug-addled
> elitist freak, and when the
> revolution comes I do not want to
> be lined up with you and shot,
> because you're fucking ripe for
> political reeducation, you know,
> like in the fields.

> FRANCIS
> Paul, let me enlighten you about
> something. You and I exist on two
> opposite sides of a great
> existential divide, that being
> your pathetic virginity on the one
> hand and my astonishing number of
> sexual conquests on the other.
> You're simply jealous.

A knock at the door.

> STUDENT
> (voice off)
> Hood, telephone.

Paul gets up and opens the door.

> FRANCIS
> And remember, with your erogenous
> zones lubricated as such with the
> mighty herb, beware out there --
> because you drone on like a
> motherfucker when you're stoned.

(CONTINUED)

CONTINUED: (2)   16

>   PAUL
>   Flame on, asshole.

INT. DORM HALLWAY. NIGHT.   17

Paul walks to the pay phone at the end of the hall.

>   PAUL
>   Hello?

INTERCUT. HOOD HOUSEHOLD. NIGHT.   18

Ben Hood talks on the phone, a drink in his hand.

>   BEN
>   Paul?

In the background, we can see Wendy watching Richard Nixon on
TV. Nixon's voice drones on, occasionally filling in the
conversational interstices.

>   PAUL
>   Hi, Dad.

>   BEN
>   Hey guy. Things OK up there? You
>   all right?

>   PAUL
>   I'm fine dad.

>   BEN
>   Well good. Just confirming.
>   You'll be on the 3:50 Wednesday
>   afternoon?...Paul, you can't come
>   on Thursday because that's already
>   Thanksgiving...That's the whole
>   point of the holidays, Paul, so
>   that you and your sister can mope
>   around the house and your mother
>   and I can wait on you hand and
>   foot while the two of you
>   occasionally grunt for more food
>   from behind the hair in your
>   faces...I know it's hard for you
>   to understand, but we actually
>   enjoy it and would appreciate --

>   IN THE BACKGROUND:

>   (CONTINUED)

CONTINUED: 18

                         NIXON
                    (on TV, from San
                    Clemente press
                    conference)
          Well, with regard to the questions
          as to why Americans feel we were
          wrong to make the tapes, that is
          not particularly surprising. I
          think that most Americans do not
          like the idea of taping
          conversations and, frankly, it is
          not something that particularly
          appeals to me...

                         BEN
          Good. Thanks guy. Hold on for a
          second.
                    (turning)
          Wendy, you want to say "hi" to
          your brother?

She frowns.

                         BEN
          Come on!

She gets up sullenly and goes to the phone.

                         WENDY
          Charles.

Intercut dorm hall -- another student is waiting behind Paul for
the phone.

                         PAUL
          Charles. Have you been keeping
          out of my shit? Have you
          refrained from entering the sacred
          precincts of my room?

                         WENDY
          I have not touched your sh--
                    (looks at father)
          Stuff. You watching this?

                         PAUL
          Watching what?

                         WENDY
          Nixon, doofus! It's incredible.
          He should be shot.

                                        (CONTINUED)

CONTINUED: (2)

                      BEN
                (overhearing)
          Hey, drop the political
          assassination stuff please.

From the kitchen, Elena overhears. She's dressed to go out, but
in the process of making a Kraft macaroni and cheese dinner for
Wendy.

                    WENDY
         He's a liar!
              (still talking more to
              her father than into
              the phone)
         Dean told him on March 21st about
         Kalmback and Hunt, all about the
         payoffs to the Watergate burglars,
         so you tell me where the so-called
         "Dean Report" is, but you can't
         because it doesn't exist, because
         he lied about Haldeman and
         Erlichman and the April 17 tape,
         that's why! Liar!

Ben retreats, going to the wet bar to pour another drink.

                    BEN
              (muttering)
         OK, OK, the defense rests.
              (to Elena in the
               kitchen)
         Want another?

                    ELENA
         No thank you. We should be off.

                    BEN
         Gotcha.

He puts the bottle back down without pouring.

                              INTERCUT BACK TO PAUL:

                    PAUL
              (on the phone)
         Hey Charles. Charles, calm down
         -- I wasn't in on it.

Elena, putting on her coat, comes into the den and gives Wendy a
kiss on the forehead as Wendy mumbles her good-byes to Paul on
the phone.

                              (CONTINUED)

CONTINUED: (3)   18

                         ELENA
            Dinner's on the counter. We'll be
            at the Carvers' -- you know the
            number. (takes the phone from
            Wendy) Paul. Hi. Is there
            anything you'll want, any
            particular kind of food or snack
            or anything we can stock up on?
            ...You're all right? .... OK.
            See you next week. I love you.

Back to Paul. We see that a line has formed for the telephone.
He answers his mother self-consciously.

                         PAUL
            I do you too. I mean, me too.

The kids in line smirk.

Back to Nixon on the TV.

                         NIXON
            We must recognize that one excess
            begets another, and that the
            extremes of violence in the 1960s
            contributed to the extremes of
            Watergate...

On Wendy as she regards the TV, hearing her parents' farewells
as they leave through the front door.

                         BEN
                   (off screen)
            And Wendy! Asleep by 10 - I mean
            it young lady.

Actually, he doesn't sound much like he means it.

EXT. CARVER HOUSE. NIGHT.   19

A large New England Colonial, with a few modern additions and
touches. We hear the sound of dinner chatter.

INT. CARVER DINING ROOM. NIGHT.   20

The kitchen door swings open into the dining room, and Mikey and
Sandy Carver emerge each holding platters of food. Mikey, 15-
and-a-half, lost in space, and Sandy, 14, a sullen and barely
pubescent boy, each have towels draped over their forearms --
they are the evening's "waiters".

                                              (CONTINUED)

CONTINUED:

They move unsteadily to the table, at which sit their parents Janey (38, a hard-edged, sharp-witted beauty) and Jim (43, large and a bit goofy, a genius inventor), together with their guests, Ben and Elena Hood, and neighbors Dorothy and Ted Franklin.

We jump cut through the evening's conversations, seen mostly from the furtive POV's of the boys.

> JIM
> It was a benefit for the ACLU or
> something, and Harry Reems himself
> was there --

> DOROTHY
> The man with the -- from Deep
> Throat?

> JIM
> The very one -- something about a
> first amendment defense fund --
> well, I believe in it --

> DOROTHY
> Ted took me to see it.

> JANEY
> Ted, how romantic.

Ted just smiles. The boys' ears tingle imperceptibly.

> DOROTHY
> I have to say, the movie didn't do
> much for me. But being in that
> theater, surrounded by all those
> horny young college boys and
> perverts, there was something in
> the air that --

As this is said, Mikey accidentally spills some wine on Ben.

> BEN
> Hell! -- I mean, no problemo
> "there", Mikey. Here, I --

Janey leans over with her napkin and attempts a cursory wipe of Ben's pants. Is there a barely noticeable frisson between Ben and Janey as she removes the napkin? If there is, Elena doesn't -- or pretends not to -- notice.

> CUT TO:

INT. CARVER DINING ROOM. LATER.   21

The boys, now in pajamas (Sandy's with padded feet, Mikey's a combination of t-shirt and pj bottoms) are bringing out coffee and dessert. The adults eye Mikey's handling of the coffee pot with some nervousness.

              DOROTHY
We changed our couples group. Our
bad luck that all the other
couples in it were younger and
better looking, which was terribly
distracting for poor Ted --

              TED
Can't say as my eye didn't wander
occasionally --

              DOROTHY
And hell, if I was going to sit in
that room while they all talked
about their sexual problems and
got little Ted all hot and
bothered about --

              TED
Now we're in some geriatric group
-- though there's a couple of
lookers --

              DOROTHY
            (to Elena)
But you two are still sticking it
out with Dr. Pasmier?

              ELENA
Actually, Ben decided that, well,
I mean we both decided --

The room turns to Ben with a slightly accusatory air.

              BEN
I just don't see what the appeal
is. Like you said, Ted, people
were working themselves up --

              JIM
That's the point -- then they go
home and make up.

              (CONTINUED)

CONTINUED: 21

                         BEN
          But (puts his arm around Elena,
          who's slightly uncomfortable) --
          Elena and I, we're just not into
          all those histrionics. About the
          only big fight we've had in years
          was about whether or not to stay
          in couple's therapy!

                         JANEY
          And it appears you won.

                         ELENA
          I just thought -- Dr. Pasmier was
          so good with Wendy, when she --

                         DOROTHY
          Your daughter? She's...?

                         ELENA
          With the shoplifting, when she was
          going through that. I had her
          visit with him a few times. And
          she seemed more, well, better --
          So Ben and I talked about it, but
          I guess he's right --

                         JIM
          That's what I like about you two
          -- you seem more like good friends
          than married people.

Janey throws him a glance.

                         DOROTHY
          But then, we still don't know why
          you went to therapy in the first
          place, do we?

Uncomfortable smiles from Ben and Elena.

                                   CUT TO:

INT. CARVER LIVING ROOM. NIGHT.   22

The dinner party has moved to the living room for after-dinner
drinks. Elena remains behind to help Janey pick up the table.
She stacks a plate on top of another.

                         JANEY
          Please don't.

                                        (CONTINUED)

CONTINUED: 22

                         ELENA
              It's not a bother.

                         JANEY
              I insist.
                   (beat)
              Don't touch them.

Elena realizes that there's an edge to Janey's voice.

                         ELENA
              Oh.

                         JANEY
                   (realizing she's gone
                    too far)
              It's really quite all right.

                         ELENA
              Of course.

                                        CUT TO:

INT. CARVER LIVING ROOM. LATER.   23

The party progresses. Mikey and Sandy lie on their stomachs at
the top of the stairs, out of sight.

                         DOROTHY
              And to think -- they met at a key
              party of all things.

                         ELENA
              A key party?

                         DOROTHY
              You know, it's a California thing.
              That scuzzy husband of hers
              dragged her kicking and screaming
              to one when they were out in LA
              -- you know, the men put their car
              keys in a bowl, and then at the
              end of the evening the women line
              up and fish them out and go home
              with whoever's keys they've got.
              Anyhow, that's how she met this
              Rod person or whatever his name is
              and he's left his wife and she's
              packing for California. Irwin is
              devastated. It's so ironic.

                                        (CONTINUED)

CONTINUED: 23

                        JANEY
          Ironic?

                        DOROTHY
                  (caught out)
          Well, um, yes. Ironic. His name
          is <u>Rod</u>.

INT. CARVER FRONT HALLWAY. NIGHT.   24

The guests are leaving. The men shake hands, the women kiss,
and the men and women awkwardly peck each others' cheeks.

                        ELENA
          Thank you Janey.

                        DOROTHY
          It was lovely!

                        BEN
          Hey Jim, next time you've got to
          fill me in on whatever it is
          you're up to these days -- your
          inventions and stuff.

                        JIM
          Will do.

INT. CARVER STAIRWAY. NIGHT.   25

At the top of the stairs, a rather dejected Sandy and Mikey
finish spying on the leave-takings below. Mikey nudges Sandy,
and they silently head back down the upstairs hall.

INT. MIKEY'S ROOM. NIGHT.   26

They enter Mikey's room -- the door has a "nuclear waste --
positively no admittance" sign on it.

As Mikey reaches his bed, he doubles over, groaning, and starts
to make retching noises. He then throws himself onto the bed,
his head leaning over the far side.

Sandy walks over and sees a pile of vomit next to the bed.
Taken aback for a moment, he then reaches forward and picks it
up -- it's fake plastic vomit. He throws it on top of Mikey's
back, but Mikey doesn't take notice.

                                              (CONTINUED)

CONTINUED: 26

                         SANDY
               Stupid!
                    (pause, looking
                     sullenly at Mike's
                     back)
               Is Wendy Hood your girlfriend?

                         MIKEY
                    (not looking up, but
                     alarmed)
               Who said so?

                         SANDY
               No one.

                         MIKEY
               I don't have a girlfriend.

Mikey returns to his reading -- a copy of *The Sensuous Woman*,
obviously well pawed over. He absent-mindedly picks his nose.
As he flips the pages, a beautiful, almost electrical HUMMING
SOUND begins to fill his ears. He frowns and pauses to listen
to it.

Sandy, who has picked up a balsa wood miniature plane, obviously
doesn't hear it.

Mikey focuses on the plane as Sandy waves it through the air.
Perhaps the hum is the sound of its engines as it soars through
the sky . . .

INT. WENDY'S BEDROOM. NIGHT.   27

There is a large poster of a cartoon version of Richard Nixon --
"Tricky Dick" -- on her wall. Wendy is on the phone to her
friend Beth.

                         WENDY
               She tried to forge her mom's
               signature like a total
               retard...I've done my mom's since
               like the sixth grade...

She pauses as Beth asks a question.

                         WENDY
               Who? No way. He's like a big
               infected whitehead wearing jeans.
               I wouldn't --

She hears the downstairs door open.

                                                          (CONTINUED)

CONTINUED: 27

> WENDY
> (whispering)
> --shit, it's my parents.

She turns her light out.

INT. HOOD UPSTAIRS HALLWAY. NIGHT.   28

Ben and Elena walking past Wendy's room to their bedroom.

> BEN
> You'd think she'd learn how to
> cook a chicken, eh? My drumstick
> was still frozen when you cut
> inside there. I'm probably going
> to get whatever that disease --
> and the Franklins --

He pauses before a hall table, and, with his eyes, traces the
telephone cord under Wendy's room.

> BEN
> Hmm. I knew she'd still be up.
> Watch this --

But Elena simply continues into the master bedroom.

He starts to pull gently on the cord. And continues pulling.
No response for a few seconds. Then:

> WENDY
> (off screen, yelling
> behind her door)
> Dad, stop it!

> BEN
> Get to sleep, young lady -- and I
> mean it.

Wendy opens the door to her room.

> WENDY
> Fascist!

> BEN
> If I were a fascist I would have
> sent you to one of those Southern
> military academies a long time
> ago. Now get to bed.

She slams the door.

                                                (CONTINUED)

CONTINUED: 28

He opens it.

INT. WENDY'S BEDROOM. NIGHT.   29

Ben enters the room, angry.

                        BEN
                    Hey!

Wendy jumps into bed and under the covers, pulling them up over
her head. He stands over her, looking down at the crumpled pile
of sheet and blanket.

                        BEN
                    (softening)
                Hey, kiddo. Sleep well, huh?

He places his hand where her cheek should be, and caresses the
sheet.

                        WENDY
                    (without pulling the
                    sheet down, but
                    nicely)
                Good-night, Dad.

                        BEN
                Good night, kid.

Ben turns to the door, where he sees a silent Elena standing in
her nightgown, a slight smile on her face.

EXT. NEW CANAAN TRAIN STATION. MORNING.   30

A group of conservatively dressed commuters enter the morning
train for New York City, Ben Hood among them.

INT. TRAIN. MORNING.   31

Ben takes a seat by the window, under the emergency exit sign.

He takes out his *New York Times*, just as Janey Carver sits down
in the seat next to him.

                        BEN
                Janey Carver! I've never seen you
                on the 7:44.

                        JANEY
                Good morning, Ben.

                                              (CONTINUED)

CONTINUED: 31

> BEN
> You haven't gotten a job, or --

> JANEY
> Passport office. Didn't you hear
> Jimmy rant on about it last week?
> He wants us all to go to Africa
> this summer. The shit.

> BEN
> Sounds exciting to me.

> JANEY
> Well then I'll ask Jimmy to take
> you in my place. It's a photo
> safari, so you can take pictures
> of the animals instead of killing
> them.

> BEN
> I guess that's more ...
> ecological.

> JANEY
> Is your office mid-town or
> downtown?

> BEN
> Mid-town. Park and 52nd.

> JANEY
> Near the Mayflower Hotel?

> BEN
> I think so. Uh...

> JANEY
> I hear they have a good
> restaurant. I've just had
> breakfast but you know I'm already
> thinking about lunch.

She picks up a piece of Ben's paper and starts to read it.

EXT. MANHATTAN OFFICE BUILDING. DAY.   32

A nondescript, cleanly "modern" building. Engraved on the
doors: "Shackley and Schwimmer, Securities Brokerage --
Established 1964"

INT. SHACKLEY AND SCHWIMMER CONFERENCE ROOM. DAY.   33

Ben sits among a small group of men, which includes George
Clair, mid-thirties, unctuously handsome.

                    GEORGE
          You see Mr. Shackley, that's what
          I'm getting at -- I believe
          Forrester Industries should reduce
          its cash position -- especially
          during this period of stagflation.
          I think we can show them much
          better returns, and in the process
          earn some beefier commissions,
          if --

                    BEN
          -- But George, Mr. Shackley, I'd
          like to pause for a second, and
          ask, if it's ok, what, exactly, is
          stagflation.

                    GEORGE
          Uh, Ben --

                    BEN
          We know it's a mixture of
          inflation and stagnation. Right.
          So how should we in the securities
          industry accommodate it? Well --
          and I hope I'm not out of bounds
          here -- let's for a moment think
          of the money supply as a large
          male organ, continuously
          inflating, and yet, the societal
          vaginal cavity simply wants more.
          As the vicious circle of higher
          returns without real satisfaction
          continues, the money-organ may
          seem to be in demand, but in fact
          even the most inflated capital is
          unwanted. This is why I suggest
          that while Forrester may be lured
          by the promise of high returns, it
          should still fantasize, so to
          speak, about the safe harbor of
          capital appreciation.

The aging boss nods agreement.

                    SHACKLEY
              (more or less mumbling)
          Brilliant, brilliant.

George Clair just grins meanly.

INT. BEN HOOD'S OFFICE./ EXT. HALL. DAY.   34

Ben is gathering papers, readying to leave. He looks up to see
George Clair in his doorway.

                    GEORGE
          Hey there Benjie, you're becoming
          quite the in-house philosopher.
          When do you have time to think up
          all that stuff -- Shackley sure
          eats it up.

INTERCUT. HALL IN FRONT OF BEN HOOD'S OFFICE.

We see that Clair is deftly flirting with Hood's attractive
secretary as she is sitting in the cubicle beside the door to
his office. She looks up coyly at Clair, hidden for the moment
from Ben's view.

Ben comes out of his office, pulling on his coat. Ben vaguely
senses what's transpiring between Clair and his secretary.

                    BEN
          George, I'm just trying to get a
          global view of things -- can't
          just look at the small picture.

There's an obvious rivalry between the two of them.

                    GEORGE
          Right on, Ben. But when the old
          man retires, I bet you're going to
          have to come up with a new routine
          -- Schwimmer doesn't seem too into
          your macroeconomic thing.

                    BEN
          Thanks for the tip, George.

                    GEORGE
          No charge, Ben. Hey, you heading
          out just a little bit early today?

                    BEN
          Got a meeting uptown.

                    GEORGE
               (already moving off)
          Right on.

                                        (CONTINUED)

CONTINUED: 34

                    BEN
          Up the organization!
               (then, to himself)
          Bastard.

The secretary pretends not to hear.

INT. BOOK STORE. DAY.   35

Elena browses the self-help section. A longish-haired, slightly
gone-to-seed, but still handsome clergyman pauses next to her.
He's wearing an ecclesiastical collar and bell-bottoms.

He pulls out a copy of *Me, Myself and I*, glancing again at
Elena.

                    PHILIP
          Elena. Elena Hood, am I right?

                    ELENA
          Yes.

                    PHILIP
          Reverend Edwards. Philip Edwards.
          You came by and checked out the
          congregation a couple of times
          last year.

                    ELENA
          Yes, it was -- I ended up --

                    PHILIP
               (smiling)
          No need to make excuses -- we're
          not for everyone, I know. (beat)
          But I did think, for a time, that
          you might be someone -- What I
          mean is that you didn't seem to
          think what we were trying to do is
          laughable, like some of your
          fellow citizens around hereabouts.

                    ELENA
          No, I didn't think it laughable at
          all, I --

                    PHILIP
               (gesturing to her
               books)
          Perhaps you find in books what I
          try to find in people.

                                        (CONTINUED)

CONTINUED: 35

> ELENA
> (a pained smile)
> That sounds vaguely like an
> insult.

> PHILIP
> Oh my. I'm sorry, I didn't mean
> it that way at all. Perhaps I
> meant it simply as a -- a
> provocation.

She thinks about it, and smiles again.

EXT. NEW CANAAN HIGH SCHOOL FIELD. DAY.   36

A cool gray afternoon. A group of boys are playing flag
football on the field, while two groups of girls are gathered
underneath the bleachers at either end, warily smoking
cigarettes.

Wendy, Beth, and a couple of other girls are gathered in one
group.

> BETH
> (referring to one of
> the girls gathered in
> the other group)
> She said you licked Dave
> Brewster's weenie in the third
> floor bathroom.

> WENDY
> She's a liar. I wouldn't touch
> Dave Brewster's dick if you paid
> me. It's probably crawling with
> v.d. after he put it in her, which
> he did.

The conversation peters out at this point, as the two groups of
girls give each other the hairy eyeball from afar.

Wendy looks through from beneath the bleacher seats onto the
field where the boys are playing.

A group of boys break from a huddle, Mikey among them.

The quarterback takes the hike and Mikey runs out for a pass.
As he runs, his breathing increases in volume, filling his ears,
and transforming into the HUMMING SOUND he'd heard before.

The quarterback spots him and throws a long one.

(CONTINUED)

CONTINUED: 36

He runs in an oblivion of beautiful white sound.

The ball drops next to him as he continues, in a world of his
own, to run.

Suddenly, the humming ends and he stops and turns around, to see
all of the other kids just standing there looking at him. One
of them makes a pot-smoking gesture, as if that's the
explanation.

                    MIKEY
              (as he returns to the
              group, ball in hand)
          Did anybody hear that?

The other kids snicker. Wendy looks on, and catches Mikey's eye
for a fleeting moment.

                    WENDY
          I gotta go.

She takes hold of her bicycle and pushes off.

INT. COFFEE SHOP. DAY.   37

Elena and Philip are seated at a booth.

                    PHILIP
          It's been a tremendously
          transformative year -- maybe a
          little controversial, of course,
          but we're breaking down the old
          Unitarian barriers --

                    ELENA
          I suppose my reluctance was the
          group aspect of it -- I've never
          been much of a joiner, although I
          still consider myself a somewhat
          religious person --

                    PHILIP
          Well, I of course flatter myself
          that our church is not exactly
          what most people would call
          organized religion -- at times
          it's the disorganization that's
          liberating -- and of course I've
          begun to minister much more in
          what one might call therapeutic
          environments, in small groups, and
          one on one, couples --

                              (CONTINUED)

CONTINUED: 37

Elena looks outside the window, and sees Wendy speed past on her
bicycle.

>   ELENA
>   (cutting him off)
>   My daughter. I haven't been on a
>   bike for years.
>   (still not really
>   looking at him)
>   When was the last time you rode a
>   bike?

>   PHILIP
>   (a bit taken aback by
>   the abrupt topic
>   change)
>   They say you never forget.

>   ELENA
>   (jarred back to his
>   presence)
>   Forget what?

There's something mildly flirtatious and perhaps a bit sinister
about his manner.

>   PHILIP
>   Forget how to ride a bike.

Silence.

>   ELENA
>   No, of course you don't, you're
>   right.

EXT. FIVE AND DIME STORE. DAY.   38

Wendy pulls her bike up to the back, locks it, and walks in.

INT. FIVE AND DIME STORE. DAY.   39

Wendy moves with a certain amount of stealth through the aisles,
arriving at the candy selection.

She looks around.

She takes a package of Twinkies and slips them into the
oversized pockets of her painter's pants.

                                                    (CONTINUED)

CONTINUED: 39

She turns around, and her breath goes out of her -- an OLD WOMAN
has been watching her shoplift. The woman looks sadly at her,
but says nothing. Wendy slowly walks past her and out the back
door of the store. The woman looks on.

EXT. FIVE AND DIME STORE. DAY.   40

As she walks her bike onto the sidewalk, Wendy comes across
Sandy.

                    SANDY
          Hey, Wendy.

                    WENDY
          Hey, Sandy.

                    SANDY
          Mikey was looking for you.

                    WENDY
          Yeah? See ya.

She pushes off on her bike.

Sandy gazes after her. He takes his G.I. Joe out of his coat
pocket, and points it at her.

                    SANDY
          Bam.

EXT. SUBURBAN STREETS. DAY.   41

Wendy flies along on her bike. It's a desolately beautiful fall
day.

EXT. SILVER MEADOWS PSYCHIATRIC INSTITUTE. DAY.   42

Wendy rides by the front gates of the posh grounds of the
private psychiatric clinic. A security guard leans against a
booth.

Once a bit past the gate, she gets off her bike and walks it
into a grove of trees near the front drive.

EXT. SILVER MEADOWS. DAY.   43

Mikey is waiting amid the trees next to his bike as Wendy
arrives.

                                                     (CONTINUED)

CONTINUED: 43

                              MIKEY
                    Want some gum?

                              WENDY
                    Sure.
                         (pulling them out of
                          her pocket)
                    Twinkie?

                              MIKEY
                         (opens his mouth,
                          displaying the gum on
                          his tongue)
                    I'm chewing.

She puts the Twinkies back, and pops the gum in her mouth.

They stand together chewing.

                              WENDY
                         (after a pause)
                    Did you tell Sandy?

                              MIKEY
                    Tell Sandy? What?

Wendy doesn't say anything.

                              MIKEY
                    You didn't tell him either, did
                    you?

EXT. SILVER MEADOWS SWIMMING POOL. DAY.   44

The wind is picking up and the light is fading. Mikey and Wendy
climb the fence around the pool, which is empty and half-covered
in dead leaves and twigs.

They climb down into the concrete recess and walk into the deep
end, leaning against the far wall of the pool.

They each matter-of-factly take their gum out and put it behind
their ears.

They begin not so much to kiss as to place their tongues in each
others' mouths.

We see them from high above the pool. As the dead leaves swirl
lightly around them, Mikey gropes under Wendy's poncho.

EXT. CARVER HOUSE. DAY.   45

To establish.

INT. CARVER GUEST ROOM. DAY.   46

A couple are in the final throes of lovemaking. We see Janey
Carver's face, more or less enjoying the proceedings. The man
gives a final heave and groan, and rolls off to reveal himself
to be -- Ben Hood.

                                        JUMP CUT TO:

INT. CARVER GUESTROOM. LATER.   47

Janey smokes a cigarette. Ben is babbling.

                    BEN
          We were golfing, and you know,
          golfing to me is something I'm
          supposed to enjoy, and I was on
          the goddamn golf team in college,
          so it's something one would assume
          I do well -- I used to do well --
          but basically these days golfing
          for me is like hoeing, or plowing.

Janey smiles briefly at this.

                    BEN
          It's like farming. I am basically
          chewing up large tracts of
          expensively landscaped scenery
          with overpriced sticks, and George
          Clair has obviously, in the mere
          two years since he joined the
          firm, he has obviously been taking
          secret lessons with a golf pro,
          and I bet the entirety of his
          disposable income has been devoted
          to humiliating me on the golf
          course. And the guy talks --
          nonstop -- throughout the
          entirety of the miserable 18 holes
          -- on topics that are the supposed
          domain of my department --

                    JANEY
          Ben--

                                        (CONTINUED)

CONTINUED: 47

                              BEN
                    Yeah?

                              JANEY
                         (gently)
                    You're boring me. I have a
                    husband. I don't particularly
                    feel the need for another.

He takes a deep breath.

                              BEN
                    You have a point there. That's a
                    very good point. We're having an
                    affair. Right. An explicitly
                    sexual relationship. Your needs.
                    My needs. You're absolutely
                    right.

                              JANEY
                    You should probably get dressed.
                    The boys will be home soon.

                              BEN
                    Gotcha.

She wraps a blanket around herself and gets up.

EXT. BACK OF CARVER HOUSE. EVENING.   48

Ben cautiously walks out the back door and heads for the side
gate.

INT. HOOD KITCHEN. EVENING.   49

Wendy enters the house as Elena is finishing supper
preparations.

                              WENDY
                    Hi mom.

                              ELENA
                    Hi Wendy.

Without waiting for instructions, Wendy starts pulling out
plates and silverware and setting the table.

                              ELENA
                    I saw you on your bike today.

                                          (CONTINUED)

CONTINUED: 49

                              WENDY
                    With Mikey?

                              ELENA
                    Who?

                              WENDY
                    Nobody.

                              ELENA
                    Mikey Carver?

                              WENDY
                    We were just riding around.

Elena takes this in.

                              ELENA
                    Well, you looked very -- free --
                    when I saw you.

Wendy continues setting the table.

                              ELENA
                    Weightless almost -- as if I were
                    seeing my own memories of being a
                    girl. There was something
                    internal about it.

                              WENDY
                    Mom. Are you ok?

                              ELENA
                    Wendy, of course. I'm sorry. You
                    must think I'm ripe to be checked
                    into Silver Meadows.

                              WENDY
                    You're not a psycho!

                              ELENA
                    The people at Silver Meadows
                    aren't psychos.

                              WENDY
                    I know. They're rich drug addicts
                    and celebrities. When I saw James
                    Taylor there, and --

                                        (CONTINUED)

CONTINUED: (2)   49

                         ELENA
          We've been through this, Wendy --
          James Taylor was actually at that
          clinic up near Boston.

                         WENDY
          Well, I saw what I saw, and if you
          don't want to believe me --

                         ELENA
          Oh, Wendy.

Wendy frowns.

                         WENDY
          They need the money for my band
          uniform at school.

                         ELENA
          I thought you quit the band -- I
          never hear you practice anymore.

                         WENDY
          I don't really need to practice.
          I just play a few notes, you know,
          so I thought maybe I'd stay in.

                         ELENA
          Well, I'm sure your father and I
          would love to hear what you're
          playing these days. Maybe after
          dinner.

INT. HOOD LIVING ROOM. NIGHT.   50

Ben and Elena take their seats on the sofa. Wendy stands before
them holding an enormous trombone, with a music stand and sheet
music in front of her.

She puffs a series of seemingly disconnected notes in waltz
time.

When she's done, she looks up from the sheet music to her
parents.

They applaud.

                         BEN
          Can't wait to see how it fits in
          with all the other instruments.

                                            (CONTINUED)

CONTINUED: 50

Elena gives him a look.

INT. HOOD KITCHEN. NIGHT.   51

Elena is sorting through bills and writing checks at the kitchen
table. Ben comes in and fills a glass with ice.

               ELENA
        The Halfords have invited us again
        this year.

               BEN
      You want to go?

               ELENA
      What do you think?

               BEN
      Well, it is a neighborhood
      tradition.

He comes up behind her, looks down at the checkbook.

               BEN
      I'm, uh, going to bed.

               ELENA
      So early?

               BEN
      Rough day. Good night.

He leans over and kisses her on the cheek. She sniffs.

               ELENA
      Is that a new aftershave?

He recoils a bit.

               BEN
      Oh yeah. Musk, or something. You
      like it?

               ELENA
      Hmm. Good night.

He walks uncertainly from the room. She watches him go. Does
she know?

INT. MIKEY'S ROOM. NIGHT.   52

Mikey is painfully at work writing an English essay. Sandy
comes to the door with a geometry textbook.

                    SANDY
          Mikey?

                    MIKEY
          Yeah?

                    SANDY
          Geometry?

                    MIKEY
          Sure, anything but this English.

Sandy puts the open textbook in front of him.

                    SANDY
          Why are you so good at math but
          not in English?

                    MIKEY
          I'm not good at math. Just
          geometry.

He looks at the book.

                    MIKEY
               (drawing out his
                examples on a piece of
                paper)
          It's like, you know when they say
          "two squared"? And you think it
          means 2 times 2, equals 4? But
          really they really mean a square.
          A square with a side of two. And
          the area of the square is four.
          Like every time you use the word,
          like squared, or cubed, it's
          really space, it's not numbers,
          it's space. And it's perfect
          space, but only in your head,
          because you can't draw a perfect
          square, like in the material
          world, but in your mind, you can
          have perfect space.
               (pause)
          You know?

As Mikey goes on, we see his geometric doodles, and hear faintly
the HUMMING SOUND under his voice.

(CONTINUED)

                    SANDY
          Yeah. But I just need some help
          with my homework.

A knock at the door. Jim stands in the doorway with a suitcase
in his hand.

                    JIM
          Hey guys, I'm back.

                    MIKEY
             (honestly confused)
          You were gone?

Sandy looks at Mikey as if pondering a lost cause.

                    JIM
             (a look of
               disappointment)
          Yeah, Mikey. Yep, I was in
          Houston, working on some great new
          ideas about silicon, which comes
          from sand, very conductive. How
          you guys doing? How's school?

Mikey's still flustered.

                    MIKEY
          Uh, I dunno. OK, I guess.

                    JIM
          Hmm. All right!

He walks off.

                    SANDY
          You really didn't notice? Man,
          he's been gone for three days.

INT. CARVER BEDROOM. NIGHT.   53

Janey is reading, still dressed, on the bed. She nods to Jim as
he enters with his suitcase.

                    JANEY
          Good trip?

He nods and puts his suitcase down, then sits heavily on the
side of the bed.

                                (CONTINUED)

CONTINUED: 53

           JIM
        (as he sits)
   You bet.

It turns out it's a water bed, and his weight creates a wave
that nearly pushes Janey off her edge of the bed.

          JANEY
   Jesus, Jim!

           JIM
        (jumping up, which only
         creates another wave)
   Sorry honey. Hell, we've got to
   trade this thing in for a normal
   bed.

          JANEY
   Just be careful.

           JIM
        (as he begins to
         unpack)
   You notice anything with Mikey
   lately? The kid seemed a little
   out of it tonight, eh?

          JANEY
   Tonight? Jim, he's been out of it
   since he was born.

           JIM
   Hell, I guess he takes after me,
   huh?

He laughs to himself.

She gives him a look.

INT. COFFEE SHOP. DAY.   54

Elena and Philip Edwards are having coffee again.

          PHILIP
   In many ways, the church-bound
   tradition of the father, son, and
   holy ghost is simply a version of
   the parent-child-adult triad
   within us all. It's a primitive
   set of symbols for our inner
   psychology.

(CONTINUED)

                    ELENA
          You're saying that Christ is the
          child, and --

                    PHILIP
          -- And God the angry parent, and
          the Spirit the hope of an
          integrated adult self.

                    ELENA
          All well and good -- But tell me
          again what it is exactly that you
          believe in?

                    PHILIP
          You ask what the point is?

                    ELENA
          That's right.

                    PHILIP
          Self-realization. Ministering to
          help people reach their fullest
          potential. Would you believe me
          if I told you I want you to see
          yourself reach your fullest
          potential and self-realization?

                    ELENA
               (pause)
          I would say it sounds like you're
          trying to get me into bed.

                    PHILIP
          If that's a potential you see
          yourself fulfilling...I mean...
               (flustered) My, I sound a bit --

                    ELENA
          I'm sorry. That was stupid of me.
          I didn't mean to be so rude.

                    PHILIP
          You weren't. You actually, for
          some reason, you have the effect
          of making me feel just a tiny bit
          ashamed of myself.

                    ELENA
          But not too ashamed.

(CONTINUED)

CONTINUED: (2)

> PHILIP
> (smiling)
> Now you are being rude.

> ELENA
> And you're still trying to get me
> into bed.

> PHILIP
> Ouch.

Just then, Dorothy Franklin passes by their table, a smirk
firmly implanted on her face.

> DOROTHY
> Hello you two. Am I barging in on
> some kind of religious study
> group? Elena, you look marvelous.
> Will I see you and Ben at the
> Halford's?

> ELENA
> I suppose we'll make an
> appearance.

> DOROTHY
> And Reverend Edwards? Did you
> make the list?

> PHILIP
> (laughing)
> I believe so Mrs. Franklin.

> DOROTHY
> With the two of you there it will
> be positively a revival! I'm off!

She scurries out of the coffee shop.

> PHILIP
> I'm afraid she's something of a
> gossip, isn't she?

> ELENA
> (gathering her things
> to go)
> I'm afraid people around here
> provide her with quite a bit to
> gossip about. (getting up) Take
> care.

(CONTINUED)

CONTINUED: (3)   54

                        PHILIP
                  (watching her go)
               That I will indeed.

INT. CLASSROOM. DAY.   55

Mikey is reading his English paper before the class.

                        MIKEY
               Because of molecules we are
               connected to the outside world
               from our bodies. Like when you
               smell things, because when you
               smell a smell it's not really a
               smell, it's a part of the object
               that has come off of it --
               molecules. So when you smell
               something bad, it's like in a way
               you're eating it.   This is why
               you should not really smell
               things, in the same way that you
               don't eat everything in the world
               around you -- because as a smell,
               it gets inside of you. So the
               next time you go into the bathroom
               after someone else has been there,
               remember what kinds of molecules
               you are in fact eating.

An embarrassed silence.

INT. SCHOOL MUSIC ROOM. DAY.   56

Band practice.   The New Canaan High School band plays a wind
version of a popular rock tune.

In front, there's Wendy, in halter top and hip-hugging bell
bottoms, incongruously blowing away on her trombone -- this
being her one stab at extracurricular activities.

In the flute section directly behind her is Sandy, piping away
on a tiny piccolo. He sits on a riser slightly elevated above
her.

He directs downward at Wendy a protracted regard, a look of
intense concentration on his face.

                        (CONTINUED)

CONTINUED: 56

SANDY'S POV:

Wendy's backside, her pants pushed outward in the back,
affording Sandy a libido-charged view of the top of her bum
crack.

Push in on a close-up of this cherished abstract landscape, then
back to Sandy's furrowed face.

INT. HOOD DEN. DAY.   57

Elena sits in a yoga pose. She opens her eyes and lets her
limbs relax.

INT. HOOD GARAGE. DAY.   58

Elena enters the garage from the kitchen and turns the light on.

She finds an old bicycle and pulls it out.

EXT. SUBURBAN STREETS. DAY.   59

Elena rides her bike into town, infused with the girlish sense
of freedom she imagined for her daughter.

Suddenly, there's a pop -- a tire is blown out. She slows down
and gets off the bike.

EXT. SUBURBAN STREETS. LATER.   60

She walks with the bike, as a station wagon slows near her. The
driver's side window rolls open. It's Janey Carver.

                    JANEY
              Need a lift?

INT. JANEY'S CAR. DAY.   61

Elena sits in the passenger seat. The two women are obviously
uncomfortable with each other.

Silence.

                    ELENA
              Thanks again. For the dinner.

                                        (CONTINUED)

CONTINUED: 61

                         JANEY
               Thanks for eating it. I don't
               know why I even pretend I can
               cook.

                         ELENA
               I used to know how to cook.

                         JANEY
               It's not like we're too busy.

They smile, barely.

                         ELENA
               I'm thinking of going back to
               school.

                         JANEY
               Social work?

                         ELENA
               How'd you know?

                         JANEY
               Educated guess.

                         ELENA
               I'm that predictable? No, you
               don't have to answer that. It's
               just that with the kids almost
               grown --

                         JANEY
               You don't have to apologize. I'm
               too much of a cynic. You actually
               seem to be trying to figure things
               out. Don't mind me.

She pulls the car over.

EXT. FIVE AND DIME STORE. DAY.   62

Janey's car pulls to the curb.

INT. JANEY'S CAR. CONT'D.

                         JANEY
               Here you are.

                                        (CONTINUED)

CONTINUED: 63

                          ELENA
                    (opening her door)
               Thanks for the lift. If the
               bike's any bother--

                          JANEY
               None at all. I'll leave it in
               front of your garage. Happy
               Thanksgiving.

EXT. FIVE AND DIME. CONT'D.   64

Elena watches the car pull away. She turns and walks into the
store.

INT. FIVE AND DIME. DAY.   65

Elena moves through the aisles, putting various sundries into a
basket.

She pauses in front of the lipsticks.

She picks up a lipstick, looks at it, then quietly places it in
her pocketbook. She puts the basket down on an empty aisle
shelf.

We see her reflection in the security mirror above the aisle, as
she quickly exits the store.

The middle-aged lady behind the counter watches her leave.

EXT. FIVE AND DIME. DAY.   66

In a wide shot, from across the street, we see Elena leave the
store, followed by the shopkeeper who runs behind her and taps
her on the shoulder. They converse for a minute, and Elena is
accompanied back into the store.

Through the store windows we see her take the lipstick out of
her purse. She's obviously distraught -- offering to pay,
talking quickly, etc. The shopkeeper is holding a telephone, not
yet decided on whether to call her in.

                                        (CONTINUED)

CONTINUED: 66

> PAUL
> (voice over)
> To find yourself in the Negative
> Zone, as the Fantastic Four often
> do, means that all everyday
> assumptions are inverted -- even
> the invisible girl herself becomes
> visible, and so she loses the last
> semblance of her power.

EXT. TRAIN. DAY. 67

As it moves through the gray afternoon landscape.

INT. TRAIN. DAY. 68

Close on images from The Fantastic Four.

> "HERE IN THE NEGATIVE ZONE, HIS
> POWERS ARE HALVED. WE CAN DO
> NOTHING BUT WAIT...AND *PRAY*" "BUT
> WHAT ABOUT *FRANKLIN*? *HE'LL BE
> KILLED*!"

Paul sits reading on his way home.

EXT. CARVER HOUSE. DAY. 69

Janey pulls up in the driveway. As she gets out of the car, she hears a small explosion from the back of the house.

EXT. CARVER BACKYARD. DAY. 70

Janey comes around the back to discover Sandy stuffing a model airplane with m-80 firecrackers. He lights them and runs back a safe distance. The plane explodes, its wreckage joining the debris from a few other dolls, models, and toys.

> JANEY
> Sandy!

Sandy looks up -- busted.

Janey marches over to him.

(CONTINUED)

CONTINUED:

                    JANEY
       You little idiotic prick, you
       could blow yourself fucking sky
       high with all this demented crap.

Sandy looks on the verge of tears. She softens and bends down
to him.

                    JANEY
         (sighing)
   Hey.
         (picking up the
          firecrackers)
   I'll take this stuff.

                    SANDY
   You going to tell dad?

                    JANEY
   Would it matter?
         (sees something else
          lying on the ground)
   And what's that?

                    SANDY
         (sniffling)
   You know, it's the whip -- the one
   uncle Frank got me from Mexico.

                    JANEY
   It's not packed with explosives,
   is it?

                    SANDY
   No!

                    JANEY
         (going into the house)
   Play with the whip.

INT. CARVER LIVING ROOM. DAY.   71

Mikey and Wendy are in front of the TV, watching a rerun of
Divorce Court.

                    JANEY
   Oh. Hi, Wendy.

                    WENDY
   Hi, Mrs. Carver.

                           (CONTINUED)

                           JANEY
              Mikey, have you heard the
              explosions coming from the
              backyard?
                    (he stares blankly at
                    her)
              Do you know what Sandy's been up
              to?

                          MIKEY
                    (honestly oblivious, as
                    usual)
              I dunno.

She pauses, then walks into the kitchen.

EXT. CARVER BACKYARD. DAY.   72

Sandy flicks his enormous whip in the direction of a small bush.

One by one, he snaps off its leaves.

INT. CARVER KITCHEN. DAY.   73

Janey hauls a turkey out of a bag and into the fridge.

INT. CARVER LIVING ROOM. DAY.   74

Mikey and Wendy are still in front of the TV.

Janey comes in again and looks at them.

                           JANEY
              Excuse me. Don't you kids have
              homework?

                     MIKEY AND WENDY
                    (without looking up, in
                    unison)
              Thanksgiving break.

She walks out of the room again.

Sandy comes in, whip in hand, looks over at Mikey and Wendy,
then walks over to them, and, without a word, slumps down beside
them and watches the TV.

EXT. TOWN STREET. DAY.   75

Elena walks unsteadily, pausing to rest against a brick wall.
She takes a deep breath, then walks to a corner where a local
taxi station wagon sits idling. She gestures to the driver, who
beckons her in.

INT. CARVER LIVING ROOM. DAY.   76

Later, Sandy, Mikey, and Wendy still mentally devolve in front
of the TV, but with various junk food detritus surrounding them
and a different show, a rerun of the original *Highway Patrol*.

Sandy wanders off.

                              CUT TO:

INT. CARVER LIVING ROOM / STAIRS / BATHROOM. LATER.   77

Wendy gets up, goes upstairs, and wanders down the hall to the
bathroom.

She gets to the door just as Sandy gets there from the opposite
direction.

                    WENDY
          After you.

Sandy hesitantly opens the door, as Wendy still hovers by it.

                    SANDY
          Well, you can....

                    WENDY
          Hey Sandy, what were you blowing
          up out there? Your mom was pretty
          p.o.'d.

                    SANDY
          All my model planes.

                    WENDY
          The ones you built?

                    SANDY
          They were old. And they couldn't
          fly anyhow. I'm going to get a
          radio-controlled airplane at
          Christmas, and then I'll stuff it
          full of m-80s and fly it into Mrs.
          Burgess's English class and blow
          it up.

                              (CONTINUED)

CONTINUED: 77

>   WENDY
>   I have to go to the bathroom.

>   SANDY
>   Yeah.

But he stays put, unaware it seems that he's blocking the
doorway.

Wendy looks around -- no one in sight.

>   WENDY
>   I'll show you mine if you show me
>   yours.

Sandy goes wide-eyed, and almost against his will backs into the
bathroom like a feather.

INT. CARVER LIVING ROOM. DAY.   78

Mikey looks up from the TV, wondering where Wendy is. He eats
another Pringle.

INT. CARVER BATHROOM. DAY.   79

Wendy flips up her dress for Sandy.

He slowly unzips, his hand unsteady. We can tell from the look
on Wendy's face that she's feeling a bit sorry for the little
guy.

Suddenly Sandy turns beet red, and bursts into tears.

>   SANDY
>   What do you want?! What do you
>   want? Get out! Get out of here!

The door flips open -- and Janey Carver appears.

>   JANEY
>   (sizing up the
>   situation)
>   Shit.

INT. MASTER BEDROOM. DAY.   80

Janey is giving Wendy a lecture.

>   (CONTINUED)

CONTINUED: 80

                        JANEY
          A person's body is his temple,
          Wendy. This body is your first
          and last possession. Now as your
          own parents have probably told
          you, in adolescence our bodies
          tend to betray us. That's why, in
          Samoa and in other developing
          nations, adolescents are sent out
          into the woods, unarmed, and they
          don't come back until they've
          learned a thing or two. Do you
          understand?

INT. CARVER HOUSE DOORWAY. DAY.   81

Wendy is led to the door by Mrs. Carver.

Wendy trades a glance with a sullen Mikey, who sits in the
living room pretending to ignore her.

EXT. STREET. DAY.   82

Wendy walks her bike with the wind in her face.

Mikey rides up alongside her on his bike.

She doesn't look at him.

Trying to stay on his bike, but moving slowly, he wobbles,
nearly falling off.

                        MIKEY
          I don't ever want to see you.

                        WENDY
          Then why'd you come after me?

EXT. HOOD HOUSE. DAY.   83

The taxi pulls up. Elena gets out and pays the driver.

INT. HOOD KITCHEN. DAY.   84

Ben is in front of the open freezer, trying to get something
out. He hears Elena come in the front door.

                                              (CONTINUED)

                              BEN
                    Elena. I need some help here if
                    this thing's gonna defrost by
                    tomorrow.

She comes up and together they tug and pull until they succeed
in extracting a large, frozen turkey. As they pull it out, it
slips from their hands and, after a dull thump, slides along the
floor.

They smile.

Elena bends over to pick it up. Ben observes her. She notices
his look.

                              BEN
                    Here.

He goes over and picks up the turkey, placing it in the sink.
He looks back at her and notices her vaguely distraught look.

                              BEN
                    You all right there?

                              ELENA
                    Oh. Sure, I -- Did you remember
                    to pick up the cranberry sauce?

                              BEN
                    Um, yes.

They stand together, his concern and her vulnerability forming
an awkward attraction between them.

                              ELENA
                    Because you like it on your turkey
                    sandwiches.

                              BEN
                    I do. I'm -- are you...?

                              ELENA
                    I...I think I...

                              BEN
                         (pause)
                    You know Elena, I've been
                    thinking --

                              ELENA
                    Ben, maybe no talking right now?
                    If you start talking, you're going
                    to --

CONTINUED: (2)   84

She kisses him as if she needs him.

INT. HOOD HALLWAY. DAY.   85

Ben and Elena enter their bedroom. Elena closes the door
quietly behind her.

INT. HOOD BEDROOM. DAY.   86

Ben and Elena undress shyly.

They make love. Elena's face is almost fearful.

                                        CUT TO:

INT. HOOD BEDROOM. LATER.   87

Elena and Ben lie in bed side by side in the pale afternoon
light.

                    BEN
              Wow. You kind of forget what
              you're missing...

He gets up and starts to get dressed.

                    BEN
              I should probably be getting
              going, to get Paul.

He smells the armpits of the shirt he's putting on.

                    BEN
              Yikes -- I was hoping to wear this
              thing to the Halford's Friday.

He looks at Elena, and realizes she's started to cry.

                    BEN
              Hey. Elena?

                    ELENA
              It's nothing.

                    BEN
              What? What is it?

                    ELENA
              That shirt?

                                        (CONTINUED)

CONTINUED: 87

                   BEN
       What?

                  ELENA
       Leave it -- I'll wash it for you.

He looks at her ruefully.

EXT. HOOD STREET. DAY.   88

Wendy walks and Mikey rides along.

                 WENDY
       You have to follow me?

                 MIKEY
       I dunno. I --

They're now in front of the Hood's house.

EXT. HOOD HOUSE. DAY.   89

Ben exits the house in a rush, and sees Wendy and Mikey on the
street in front.

                 BEN
       Hey, there Mikey, how's business?

                 MIKEY
         (tripping off of his
         bike)
       Business? Uh, I dunno.

Ben grimaces, fiddles for his car keys.

As Mikey remounts and rides off, Wendy passes her father on the
driveway.

                 BEN
       I'm picking up Paul at the station
       -- want to come?

                 WENDY
       Nah.

                 BEN
       What you been up to?

(CONTINUED)

CONTINUED: 89

> WENDY
> Nothing.

EXT. STREET. DAY.   90

Mikey rides slowly home. At a lonely bend in the road, he
wobbles again on his bike and falls off.

> MIKEY
> Jeez.

He stands and dusts himself off, humiliated, alone.

Motionless, rooted to the spot, a wave of awful sentiment and
fear overcomes him. He shudders at the barely audible sensation
of the now-familiar hum.

INT. HOOD LIVING ROOM. DAY.   91

Wendy enters the house and climbs the stairs.

She sees the crumpled bed sheets in her parents' room and hears
Elena in the shower.

EXT. NEW CANAAN STATION. DAY.   92

Paul walks to the parking lot with his father, who carries his
duffel bag.

EXT. STREETS. DAY.   93

Ben's car heading back to the house with Paul.

INT. HOOD CAR. DAY.   94

> BEN
> So how's school treating you?

> PAUL
> All right.

> BEN
> Classes?

> PAUL
> Good.

(CONTINUED)

CONTINUED: 94

                          BEN
              Grades?

                          PAUL
              Fine.

                          BEN
              Anyone special? You know...

                          PAUL
              Hnnn.

                          BEN
              Well it's good to see you -- we
              miss you around the house and all,
              but this St. Peter's, it's top of
              the line, eh?

                          PAUL
              Yeah.

                          BEN
              You know Paul, I've been thinking,
              maybe this is as good a time as
              any to have a little talk, you
              know, about -- well --

He makes a sharp turn. Paul puts his arms up on the dashboard
to steady himself.

                          PAUL
                     (nervous)
              About?

                          BEN
              Well, the whole gamut. Facts of
              life and all. Some fatherly
              advice, because, I tell you,
              there's things happening that
              you're probably old enough
              to...digest.

                          PAUL
              Uh...things?

Ben hesitates.

                          BEN (Cont'd)
              Well... things that happen between
              a...
                     (pause)
                        (more)

                                              (CONTINUED)

CONTINUED: (2)   94

> BEN (Cont'd)
> For example, on the self-abuse
> front -- and this is important --
> it's not advisable to do it in the
> shower -- it wastes water and
> electricity and because we all
> expect you to be doing it there in
> any case -- and, um, not onto the
> linen, and not on your sister's
> underwear or any clothing
> belonging to your mother --

He pauses to gauge the effect of his monologue on his son, then
continues.

> PAUL
> Uh, Dad --

Just then Ben runs a stop sign and almost slams into another
car.

> BEN
> Holy! Well. If you're worried
> about anything, just feel free to
> ask, and, uh, we can look it up.

> PAUL
> Uh, Dad, you know I'm 16.

> BEN
> All the more reason for this
> little heart-to-heart...great.

They drive up to the house.

> BEN
> Um, Paul?...On second thought...

EXT. HOOD HOUSE. DAY.   95

The car pulls up and parks.

> BEN
> I was thinking, can you do me a
> favor and pretend I never said any
> of that.

> PAUL
> Sure, Dad.

(CONTINUED)

CONTINUED: 95

                    BEN
          Thanks.

Paul gets out, looking shell-shocked. He sees Wendy waving to
him from a second floor window. He nods back.

In the doorway, Elena waits.

INT. HOOD HALLWAY. DAY.   96

Paul knocks on Wendy's bedroom door. She opens it.

                    PAUL
          Hello, Charles.

                    WENDY
          Greetings, Charles.

INT. WENDY'S ROOM. DAY.   97

Paul and Wendy sit on the floor.

                    PAUL
          How are the parental units
          functioning these days?

                    WENDY
          Dad's like doing his Up With
          People routine, Mom hasn't been
          saying much.

                    PAUL
          I don't know. Dad seems a little
          weird. You know, nervous.

                    WENDY
          Yeah, well, wait till Mom finally
          opens her mouth.

They both ponder silently. Then:

                    PAUL
          You think they're headed for,
          like, the dustbin of history?

                    WENDY
          Huh?

                    PAUL
          Divorce court?

                                              (CONTINUED)

CONTINUED:

                    WENDY
        They dropped out of their couples
        group therapy thing.

                    PAUL
        Is that good or bad?

She just shrugs. Silence. Then:

                    PAUL
        May I operate the telephonic
        apparatus?

                    WENDY
        Why don't you use the phone
        downstairs?

                    PAUL
        Calling an individual, Charles, in
        New York. Confirming a social
        outing for Friday night.

                    WENDY
        Can I come?

                    PAUL
        It's a one-on-one kind of date
        thing.

                    WENDY
        With who?

                    PAUL
        Her name's Libbets.

                    WENDY
        Libbets? What kind of a name is
        Libbets?

The record they've been listening begins to skip.

                    PAUL
        Hey, is that my record?

                    WENDY
        It skipped from before I borrowed
        it.

Paul goes and takes the record off the stereo.

                         (CONTINUED)

CONTINUED: (2)   97

                         PAUL
             You have messed with my shit,
             Charles.

He looks at her and shrugs -- he doesn't really mind.

EXT. HOOD HOUSE. DAY.   98

Morning. To establish.

INT. HOOD BEDROOM. DAY.   99

Elena is coming out of the master bathroom in a robe, a towel
wrapped around her head.

                         ELENA
             The turkey in?

                         BEN
             Stuffed and roasting.

INT. HOOD HALLWAY. DAY.   100

Ben Hood pads down the hall in his bathrobe, tries the bathroom
door. It's locked.

                         BEN
             Anyone home?

INT. HOOD BATHROOM. DAY.   101

The shower is running, but Paul is standing by the open window,
puffing on a joint and trying to blow the smoke outside.

                         PAUL
             I'll be out in a second.

Ben walks back to the bedroom, smirking.

                         BEN
             Sure you will.

INT. PAUL'S ROOM. DAY.   102

Paul is standing on the bed, taking his old sports posters down
from the wall.

                              (CONTINUED)

CONTINUED: 102

Elena comes to the door.

                    ELENA
          Supper's almost ready...Maybe you
          want to save those?

                    PAUL
          They've been up for too long.

                    ELENA
          You've lost your interest in
          sports?

                    PAUL
          No...just, you know, professional
          sports, opium for the masses kind
          of thing, though I'm into
          intramural, you know, less
          competitive, participation --

                    ELENA
               (smiling)
          I see.

                    PAUL
          You know, like frisbee.

Even Paul has to laugh at himself. Elena joins him.

A beat.

                    PAUL
          Um, Mom, you know Wendy was
          saying, that you and Dad...

                    ELENA
          Wendy said what?

                    PAUL
          Something about therapy?

                    ELENA
          Oh that. Well, your father and I
          thought it might help...with our
          communicating? And I think it
          did.

                    PAUL
          So you and Dad are...
          communicating?

Elena smiles reassuringly.

                                        (CONTINUED)

                        ELENA
Sure.

As she leaves he room, her smile fades.

INT. HOOD DINING ROOM. DAY.   103

One by one, each member of the Hood family carries in a final
item to place on the overstuffed Thanksgiving table. Then, one
by one, they each silently take their seats.

They look over the table. No one moves.

                        BEN
Well, it's great we can all be
together. And this Thanksgiving,
no hysteria, no yelling,
especially with grandpa not here,
although we miss him. So let's do
it right and actually, Wendy, why
don't you say grace. You used to
love to say grace, remember?

Wendy grimaces, as they all bow their heads slightly.

                        WENDY
Dear Lord, thank you for this
Thanksgiving holiday, and for all
the material possessions that we
have and enjoy, and for letting us
white people kill all the
Indians...

Everyone looks up.

                        WENDY
... and steal their tribal lands
and stuff ourselves like pigs ...

Mutterings and groans: "Wendy!" "For Christ's sake" etc.

                        WENDY
... while children in Africa and
Asia are napalmed and --

                        BEN
Jesus! All right, enough! Paul
-- gravy?

                          (CONTINUED)

CONTINUED: 103

They all unceremoniously start to dig in.

                                          FADE OUT:

EXT. CARVER HOUSE. DAY.   104

To establish.

INT. CARVER GUEST ROOM / LIVING ROOM. DAY.   105

Janey Carver is pouring Benjamin Hood a drink from a bottle of
vodka. Benjamin is already unbuttoned and shoeless; Janey still
fully dressed.

                    JANEY
          Here.

                    BEN
          After the Thanksgiving I had, I
          need it. You having one?

                    JANEY
          In a bit.

She sits next to him, he kisses the back of her neck.

                    BEN
          You know, I think Elena might
          suspect something.

Janey gives him a rather contemptuous look.

                    BEN
               (thinking aloud)
          Maybe it's all for the better, you
          know? Yesterday, at dinner, well,
          she hasn't said anything...has she
          acted funny to you, I mean, have
          you noticed anything?

                    JANEY
               (almost ironic)
          Have I noticed anything? I'm not
          married to her Benjamin, you are.
          I think you've probably a better
          vantage point from which to
          observe her.

                                          (CONTINUED)

> BEN
> Yeah, but, I -- I've been working
> a lot lately, and -- No, that's
> not it. I guess we've just been
> on the verge of saying something,
> whatever it is, just saying
> something to each other. On the
> verge.

Janey gets up.

> JANEY
> I'll be back.

Benjamin looks at her quizzically.

> BEN
> Huh?

> JANEY
> Birth control.

> BEN
> Right. Gotcha.

She leaves the room.

He leans back onto the bed. Sits back up. Takes a sip of
vodka. Puts the glass down. Takes his socks off. He's now in
just his jockey shorts and shirt.

Faintly, he hears a door close. The front door?

He takes another sip.

He hears another sound.

> BEN
> Janey?

Nothing.

He goes to the door and carefully opens it.

> BEN
> (quietly)
> Janey?

He hears, quite audibly, a car door open, close, Janey's car
start and pull out.

                              (CONTINUED)

CONTINUED: (2)   105

He runs to a front window just in time to catch a glimpse of her
driving off.

               BEN
     Shit.

INT. CARVER GUEST ROOM. LATER.   106

Benjamin sits on the guest bed, still in his underwear, drinking
from the bottle.

He gets up and starts to wander around the house, still holding
the bottle.

INT. CARVER MASTER BEDROOM. CONT'D.   107

Benjamin saunters through. He presses on the king-sized bed --
it undulates.

               BEN
       Water bed! Dig it!

He wiggles comically, making more waves.

                                JUMP CUT:

Ben idly goes through Janey's drawers.

INT. CARVER MASTER BATHROOM. CONT'D.   108

He rifles through the bathroom cabinet, checking out the
medicines.

INT. CARVER BEDROOM. CONT'D.   109

He notices a garter belt hanging from the walk-in closet door.
He picks it up and twirls it.

INT. MIKEY'S ROOM. CONT'D.   110

Benjamin walks in, an obvious look of distaste.

He sorts through a few of Mike's things -- monster eyes that
glow in the dark, The Sensuous Woman, etc.

He lifts a soiled rag from under Mikey's pillow.

                            (CONTINUED)

CONTINUED: 110

                    BEN
          Yuck!

He puts it back.

He twirls the garter belt absent-mindedly, but then, thinking he
hears something downstairs, he freezes. Listening hard -- no
further sounds. He tosses the garter belt into the back of
Mike's closet, then cautiously walks out of the room.

INT. CARVER GUEST ROOM. CONT'D.   111

He finishes putting his clothes back on. As he reaches for the
door, he hears voices and quickly steps back in again.

Teenage voices. Mikey and Wendy.

                    MIKEY
                  (o.s.)
          See, no one's here. Maybe you
          want to go to the basement?

                    WENDY
                  (o.s.)
          Maybe we can just watch some TV.

                    MIKEY
                  (o.s.)
          There's a TV in the basement.

Hood hears their steps down into the basement.

INT. CARVER BASEMENT. DAY.   112

Wendy and Mikey stand in the middle of the semi-lit basement.

                    MIKEY
          Maybe we can mess around. You
          know, only if you want to...

                    WENDY
          I don't know.

                    MIKEY
          Why did you -- with Sandy?

                    WENDY
          I don't know.

                                (CONTINUED)

CONTINUED: 112

                              MIKEY
                    You like him? He worships you.

But Wendy doesn't seem to hear -- she's drawn to an object lying
next to a bean bag chair off to one side.

                              WENDY
                    Hey, what's this?

With a look of utter fascination, she picks up a Nixon mask,
looking at it as though it were an archeological find.

                              WENDY
                    Wow!

                              MIKEY
                    Wendy!

She puts the mask on.

                              WENDY
                         (from behind the mask)
                    I won't take my pants off. But
                    I'll touch it. That's as far as
                    it goes.

Mikey looks totally confused.

Remaining fully clothed, Wendy loosens Mike's belt, showing no
excitement from behind her mask, and lets him climb on top of
her for a dry hump.

Just then, a shaft of light hits them from the top of the stairs
-- Ben towers above them, looking down.

Mikey flips over immediately and pulls his clothes together,
grabbing a *TV Guide* as Wendy stands up, the mask still on.

As Ben descends, Mikey, still stuffing his shirt-tail into his
pants, pretends to flip through the *TV Guide*.

                              MIKEY
                         (muttering)
                    When worlds collide.

                              WENDY
                    Huh?

                              MIKEY
                    4:30 movie. *When Worlds Collide.*

Ben arrives, folds his arms.

                                                        (CONTINUED)

CONTINUED: (2)   112

                    BEN
What the hell are you kids doing
down here?

                    WENDY
What do you think we're doing,
Dad?

                    BEN
What do I think? I think you're
probably touching each other. I
think you're touching that
reckless jerk-off, for God's sake,
and I think he's trying to get
into your slacks. I think, at
fourteen years of age, that you're
getting ready to give up your
girlhood --

                    MIKEY
Hey, hang on there, Mr. Hood --

                    BEN
Don't you direct a single word at
me, Mikey. I don't want to hear
it. I'll be speaking with your
parents about this situation very
soon. Bet your ass on that, son.
Young lady?

                    WENDY
Talking to me, Dad?

                    BEN
Who else would I be talking to?
And take that thing off!

                    WENDY
        (pulling off the mask)
Well, then forget all this stern
dad stuff.

                    BEN
I'm not interested in your smart
ass remarks now, lady. Let's go.
Right now. You and I can discuss
it on the walk home.

She stands next to Mikey for a moment, both on the verge of
tears.

EXT. STREET. EVENING.   113

Hood and Wendy walk through a cold drizzling rain.

He looks at her from time to time, then takes her arm.

>   BEN
>   Look, kiddo, don't worry about it.
>   I really don't care that much.
>   I'm just not sure he's right for
>   you, that's all.

>   WENDY
>   Huh?

>   BEN
>   It's just that you develop a sense
>   when you get older, if things are
>   going to work out or if they
>   won't, and sometimes it's not
>   worth the mess...

She looks at him. They keep walking. She walks through a
puddle.

>   BEN
>   Your toes cold?

>   WENDY
>   Yeah.

He stops and lifts her in his arms.

>   BEN
>   I'll carry you up the drive.

She puts her arms around his neck and he lifts her up.

On her face, as he carries her -- a look of blank but real
intimacy.

INT. HOOD FRONT HALL. EVE.   114

Hood and Wendy enter, wet and cold, muttering hellos.

>   ELENA
>   (o.s., from the
>   kitchen)
>   Dinner in ten minutes.

>   BEN
>   You go dry off now.

Wendy heads for the stairs, Hood following.

INT. HOOD BEDROOM. EVE.   115

Hood finishes taking off his wet clothes as Elena enters and
turns on a light. She stands watching him.

> BEN
> Hey, should I dress for the
> Halford's now, or -- give me
> your --

> ELENA
> Up to you. I'd like to go early
> and leave pretty soon after that.

> BEN
> I get you loud and clear...hey,
> you look nice.

> ELENA
> Thanks...So where've you two been?

> BEN
> (pause)
> You'll never guess where I found
> her.

Not much response from Elena.

> ELENA
> You found her?

> BEN
> In the basement over at Janey and
> Jim's. With that weirdo Mikey.
> Not even a TV on. And they're on
> the floor and he's got his
> trousers down though thank
> goodness she's still dressed.
> Well, I really let him have it!
> (a nervous laugh)
> ...and Wendy came home
> peacefully...

> ELENA
> (pause)
> So what were you doing in the
> Carvers' basement, anyway?

> BEN
> Oh, just dropping off a coffee
> cup. Jim left it, last time he
> was over. It was on the dash of
> the car.
> (more)

CONTINUED: 115

> BEN (Cont'd)
> You were, you know, reading. I
> thought I'd just catch some air.

> ELENA
> Oh right. The mustache coffee
> cup. The one that was sitting on
> the dash.

> BEN
> Yeah, that one.

> ELENA
> That one.

She walks down to the kitchen, Benjamin following her.

INT. HOOD KITCHEN. NIGHT.   116

A silent dinner of turkey sandwiches with Elena, Benjamin, and
Wendy. The turkey carcass sits, embarrassed, in the middle of
the table.

Paul enters.

> PAUL
> See you.

> BEN
> Stay out of trouble.

> ELENA
> You'll be on the 10:30 train?

> PAUL
> 11:30?

> ELENA
> Paul --

> BEN
> Ah let the guy have his fun.
> What's the name of this girl with
> the Park Avenue address?

> PAUL
> Libbets. Libbets Casey.

> BEN
> Libbets? What kind of name is
> Libbets?

CONTINUED: 116

                         ELENA
               You'll get a taxi home from the
               station tonight? It's supposed to
               storm.

Paul shrugs and is out the door.

The meal continues.

Wendy, finished, gets up from the table. Opens the fridge, but
finds nothing. Then goes to the candy shelf and grabs some Hot
Tamales, leaving the room without a word and going into the den.

INT. HOOD DEN. NIGHT.   117

Wendy turns the TV on.

                         TV
               ... and that ends today's
               highlight coverage of the
               Watergate affair.

                         WENDY
               Shoot.

She changes the channel. A weather report is in progress.

                         WEATHERMAN
                    (on TV)
               As the cold front moves in, expect
               rapidly decreasing temperatures
               tonight, and be careful of ice on
               the roads as that downpour gets to
               freezing...

INT. HOOD KITCHEN. NIGHT.   118

Ben and Elena rise from the table with their dishes.

                         BEN
               What's for dessert?

                         ELENA
               See for yourself.

                         BEN
               No advice from the experts, huh?

His plate slips out of his hands into the trash. He fishes it
out and sets it on the counter.

                                                          (CONTINUED)

CONTINUED: 118

> ELENA
> Don't start.

> BEN
> You think I --

> ELENA
> I have no idea.

> BEN
> What's on your mind? Don't --

> ELENA
> It wouldn't make a pleasant
> evening, if that's what you're
> after. I don't want to talk about
> it. Stupid mustache cup.

> BEN
> What do you mean?

> ELENA
> Don't be dim.

INT. HOOD DEN. NIGHT.   119

Wendy puts the volume of the TV up, to drown out a conversation
she can almost overhear but doesn't want to.

INT. HOOD KITCHEN. NIGHT. CONT'D.   120

> ELENA
> Oh, lord. You think I'm so dense.
> And now you want to be seen with
> your dense wife at the cocktail
> party. You want to wear that
> ridiculous shirt which doesn't go
> with those pants at all. You want
> to wear that, and you want me to
> shake hands with your friends and
> make conversation and dress up in
> an outfit that shows a lot of
> cleavage and you're not going to
> accord me the respect of talking
> honestly about this...You don't
> really know what this feels like.

                                               (CONTINUED)

CONTINUED: 120

                    BEN
                (whispering)
        Sure I do. Do I know what
        loneliness feels like? Sure I do.
        I know a lot about it, if that's
        what you mean.

                    ELENA
        Benjamin. That's supposed to
        explain it?

                    BENJAMIN
        Explain? I didn't -- technically
        -- it's not what you're thinking
        Elena.

                    ELENA
        Please have the decency to at
        least not tell me what I'm
        thinking.

Elena sighs, then walks into the den.

INT. HOOD DEN. NIGHT.   121

                    ELENA
        We're going to the Halford's. The
        number's on the calendar in the
        kitchen. We should be home around
        11.

                    WENDY
                (eyes still glued to
                 the TV)
        Is it a big party? A big
        neighborhood party?

                    ELENA
        I suppose. Why?

                    WENDY
        Just curious. If there's a
        problem, I guess I'll just call
        you there to interrupt.

                    ELENA
        What sort of problems are you
        planning exactly?

Elena kisses the top of her head.

                                        (CONTINUED)

CONTINUED: 121

>   WENDY
>   (still watching the TV)
>   Oh, I thought I'd steal the
>   station wagon, drive up to a
>   commune. Or set the house on
>   fire. You know.

>   ELENA
>   Just bundle up. It's supposed to
>   freeze tonight. We'll see you in
>   the morning.

EXT. HOOD HOUSE. NIGHT.   122

Elena and Ben emerge from the house, and look up at a darkening,
foreboding sky. A light rain falls. They jog toward their car.

INT/EXT. HOOD CAR. NIGHT.   123

The car moves slowly through the rainy suburban streets.

Inside, Elena and Ben don't speak.

EXT. HALFORD HOUSE. NIGHT.   124

Their Firebird pulls up. There are already many other cars
parked on the lawn and driveway.

INT. HALFORD FOYER. NIGHT.   125

Ben and Elena enter. Dot Halford accosts them.

>   DOT
>   Ben, Elena. Wonderful!
>   Wonderful! So wonderful to see
>   you.

Finishing the last of a celery canoe, she kisses the air next to
Ben's ear and gives Elena a manic hug.

Then, picking up a white salad bowl from the hall table:

>   DOT
>   Would you care to play? New this
>   year.

Close on: the bowl full of keys.

                                              (CONTINUED)

CONTINUED: 125

                       DOT
       Strictly volunteer, of course.
       You can put your coats in the
       library if you like.

                     ELENA
       Oh, damn. Uh, I've left the --

                     BEN
       You've...

                     ELENA
       In the car.

                     BEN
       Oh, yeah. Yeah, we'll be right
       back, Dot.

INT/EXT. HOOD CAR. CONT'D. 126

Ben and Elena climb back in the car and close the doors,
shivering.

                     ELENA
       This just isn't the best moment
       for this.

                     BEN
       I know, I know. I had no idea --

                     ELENA
       That this was going to be a key
       party?

                     BEN
       Yeah, well, if we'd understood we
       could have invented some kind of
       excuse. A key party -- did you
       see how stuffed that bowl was
       already?

                     ELENA
       Well?

                     BEN
       I think we're here and we don't
       have to stay -- we ought simply to
       put in an appearance and then we
       can head home.

                           (CONTINUED)

CONTINUED:

                    ELENA
          Damn it, Ben --

                    BEN
          I'm not staying at this party so
          we can go home with someone else's
          wife. That's not why we're here,
          right? We're simply being
          neighbors here, and I think we
          should do just that --

                    ELENA
          You're not going to --

                    BEN
          I'm not.

                    ELENA
          You have some marker, that's what
          I think, if you want to know the
          truth. You have some marker and
          you're going to put it on the
          house keys so that Janey can find
          them and then when I get back to
          the house I'll find the two of you
          in there and Wendy'll be able to
          hear you and Paul will be back and
          he'll hear you and I'll catch you,
          that's what I think. She'll be
          swearing and banging against the
          wall and I'll catch --

                    BEN
          Elena.

She rubs her eyes.

                    BEN
          Elena, it's not what you think.
          It's not a big plot. Honestly.
          Honestly. I don't know if you
          want to go over this now, but it's
          just something that comes over me.
          I don't feel good about it. I
          know I've done what I didn't want
          to do. I don't know --

                    ELENA
          Well, I'm really pleased to hear a
          confession.

                                        (CONTINUED)

CONTINUED: (2)   126

                         BEN
             Elena, you're just getting wound
             up to get wound up.

                         ELENA
             Thanks for the diagnosis, Ben.
             Thank you. So let's just go to
             this fiasco if that's what you
             want to do. Let's just go on in.
             I'd rather talk to anyone else but
             you.

She pulls the keys out of the ignition, gets out of the car, and
slams the door. He follows her.

INT. HALFORD FOYER. NIGHT.   127

                         ELENA
             Oh, Dot!

Elena, entering the house again, tosses the keys at Dot Halford,
who looks surprised.

Ben slides in behind his wife.

Dot drops the keys into the bowl.

Slow-motion, close up: the keys, on their equine chain, fall in
with a THUNDEROUS CRASH.

INT. HALFORD LIVING ROOM. CONT'D.   128

The room is crowded with nervous, expectant couples and various
groupings.

Elena slips into a side room.

Benjamin heads over immediately to the drink table and pours a
stiff one, turning around to find at his elbow none other than
George Clair.

                         GEORGE
             Benjie!

                         BEN
             Clair, George Clair! What the
             hell brings you to New Canaan?

                                        (CONTINUED)

CONTINUED:

> GEORGE
> Well, it's the funniest thing.
> I've been talking to some
> investors -- a little outside
> venture, you understand, between
> you and me -- about a scheme to
> manufacture a new Styrofoam
> packaging. Little peanut-like
> pieces that can really keep an
> item free from trauma during
> shipping. Miraculous. Anyway, it
> turns out the genius behind the
> whole project is your neighbor,
> Jim Carver. How about that!

> BEN
> Well, hey, isn't that a one-in-a-
> million coincidence. A real
> dreamer, Jim Carver, eh?

> GEORGE
> Darned right. Look here, Benj,
> whaddya make of this sequel to *The
> Godfather?* You think it's gonna
> work?

> BEN
> Don't see how. I think the
> public's had its fill of this
> gangster stuff. No, trust me --
> disaster pics. And air hockey.

> GEORGE
> Yeah, good.

Benjamin catches a glimpse of Janey, voluptuously attired, across the room.

> GEORGE
> Well, gonna make a break for the
> hors d'oeuvres guy.

> BEN
> Yeah, see you bright and early
> Monday A.M.
>   (beat)
> Say, where's the wife?

> GEORGE
> (winking as he goes)
> In Rhode Island with the folks.
> I'm a free agent tonight.

(CONTINUED)

CONTINUED: (2)   128

At this, they both notice Elena slowly gliding across the other
side of the room. Clair gives Ben a sideways glance, then moves
on.

Ben makes straight for Janey, who pretends to be preoccupied
with a plant.

                    JANEY
          Oh jeez, Benjie. Well, here you
          are.

                    BEN
          Damn right, but where the hell
          were you?

                    JANEY
               (looking around)
          What are you talking about?

                    BEN
               (whispering, but too
                loudly)
          Don't bullshit me around, Janey.
          Jesus Christ, I waited around for
          more than half an hour, in nothing
          but my boxer shorts, and -- and
          what's all that about? What the
          hell happened?

Janey takes a sip of her drink.

                    JANEY
          A prior engagement overcame me.

                    BEN
          What?

                    JANEY
          Listen, Benjamin Hood. I have
          obligations that precede your. . .
          from before you showed up. One or
          two, you know, good-natured
          encounters, that doesn't mean I'm
          . . . I'm not just some toy for
          you. When I remembered some
          chores I wanted to get done before
          the party, I just did them, that's
          all, because I wanted to do them
          before I saw Jimmy.

                              (CONTINUED)

CONTINUED: (3)   128

                         BEN
          Jimmy? Jimmy? I don't know how
          to take this. And what do you
          mean, Jimmy? I thought you said
          you and your husband --

                         JANEY
          How you take it isn't all that
          interesting to me, Benjamin. I'm
          sorry --

                         BEN
          I just can't believe you could be
          so --

Stalling, he watches her take another sip of her drink and
wander off.

The air is filled with talk of Watergate, Billie Jean King, the
Oil Crisis, the Mets.

Benjamin goes over to the couch, where Dave Gorman is chatting
up an attractive younger woman.

                         GORMAN
                    (lighting up a joint)
          Welcome to the Monkey House has
          been a seminal influence on me --
          hey Benjamin -- give it a try?
          This stuff will make some sense
          out of those larger questions.

                         BEN
                    (waving it away)
          Thanks for the advice Dave.

But then, Benjamin changes his mind.

                         BEN
          Uh, well, what the hey...

Taking he joint, he tugs on it, holding the smoke in his lungs.

                         BEN
                    (coughing)
          Good shit.

                         GORMAN
          Sure is good shit. It's opiated.
          I had it in my chamber for a
          while. I was smoking this
          other --

                                             (CONTINUED)

CONTINUED: (4)   128

                    BEN
          It's what?

                       GORMAN
          Don't fret, Benjie, it's --

                    BEN
          Darn it, Dave.

He rises unsteadily, weaving through the room's conversations.

                    JACK MOELLERING
          Take California. They've got
          their own airline in-state that's
          not subject to the fare controls.
          Compare Sacramento to LA on the
          controlled airlines and you'll see
          what Friedman is saying -- supply
          and demand, less restriction.

Benjamin walks over to a window. The outdoor lamps illuminate a
new and heavy downpour of frozen sleet.

INT. CONRAIL TRAIN. NIGHT.   129

Paul is seated, reading the latest number of *The Fantastic Four*
comic book. The cover displays a lurid, atomically glowing
baby.

The conductor walks through the cabin.

                    CONDUCTOR
          Approaching our final stop, Grand
          Central Station.

Paul looks out the window at the tenements of Harlem, barely
visible through the walls of sleet. Soon the train enters the
tunnel toward the station.

EXT. PARK AVENUE APARTMENT BUILDING. NIGHT.   130

Paul gets out of a cab and heads inside. He's met by the
doorman.

                    PAUL
          Libbets Casey, please.

                    DOORMAN
          Your name?

                                                  (CONTINUED)

CONTINUED: 130

                    PAUL
      Paul Hood.

                    DOORMAN
          (a smirk)
      Elevator on the right. Eighth
      floor -- she's waiting for you.

INT. HALL IN FRONT OF LIBBETS' DOOR. NIGHT.   131

Paul rings the bell.

                    LIBBETS
          (o.s., from the other
          side of the door)
      Open it, Paul!

Paul opens the door, and enters the apartment.

INT. LIBBETS' APARTMENT. NIGHT.   13

It's half dark, has an air of old wealth.

Libbets skids across the parquet floor to him.

                    LIBBETS
      Excellent. We were waiting!

She turns and runs into the den.

                    PAUL
          (under his breath)
      We?

And there, in the den, cleaning an ounce of dope on an open copy
of Nixon's *Six Crises*, is -- Francis.

                    FRANCIS
          (lifting the book up)
      You oughtta read this Hood, Nixon,
      our leader, all ye need know about
      the travails of life. Check out
      the Checkers speech stuff.

                    PAUL
          (all hope drained from
          him)
      Francis. You gonna leave the
      seeds in there? In the binding
      like that?

                            (CONTINUED)

> FRANCIS
> All will be revealed, baby.

The television is turned on to a weather report about the ice storm.

> FRANCIS
> Awesome sleet and rain.

> LIBBETS
> Major.

> FRANCIS
> Hey there. You, young knight.
> Can you check on the mead? Can
> you sally forth and secure us some
> more mead?

> PAUL
> Huh?

> FRANCIS
> (nasal voice,
> impersonating a TV
> character)
> Moisture! Moisture!

> LIBBETS
> (pointing)
> Beer. In the pantry.

Paul trudges disconsolately out of the room.

INT. LIBBETS' KITCHEN. NIGHT   133

Paul, after wandering a maze of halls, enters the kitchen, where he takes a six-pack out of the fridge and returns to the living room.

INT. LIBBETS' LIVING ROOM. NIGHT   134

He enters the room with the beer.

> LIBBETS
> Frankie opens them with his teeth.

> PAUL
> (handing him a beer)
> Hey, it's a sellable skill.

(CONTINUED)

134

Francis licks closed a second joint, then takes the beer and
opens it with his rear molars.

> FRANCIS
> Hell on the fillings.

Paul opens the other two beers and hands one to Libbets. They
light up a joint.

> FRANCIS
> Everything's gonna freeze, the big
> freeze.

> LIBBETS
> Yeah, Paul, are you gonna get home
> okay?

Paul and Francis exchange a look.

She puts an Allman Brothers tape on the 8-track and turns the TV
down.

INT. HOOD HOUSE. NIGHT.   135

Wendy wanders desultorily through the house. She walks into her
parents' bedroom and lies down on the bed. She sticks her legs
up into the air for a few seconds, then lets them down. She
gets back up and walks into the hall.

INT. HOOD BATHROOM. NIGHT.   136

Wendy enters the bathroom.

She fills the sink with water, then turns off the tap. She
takes a razor blade from the counter, and slowly, determinedly,
holds it to her wrist.

She presses it into her skin, drawing a small drop of blood.

> WENDY
> Ouch!

She drops the blade and splashes water on her wrist, grabbing
some toilet paper and holding it against the tiny wound.

> WENDY
> Stupid.

She hears the phone ring and walks downstairs.

INT. HOOD DEN. NIGHT.   137

Wendy picks up the phone.

                    WENDY
              Hood residence.

INT. CARVER KITCHEN. NIGHT.   138

Mikey is on the other end of the line.

                    MIKEY
              Your parents at that party?

                                        INTERCUT:

                    WENDY
              Yeah. Yours?

                    MIKEY
              You get in trouble?

                    WENDY
              Maybe. Can't really tell yet.

                    MIKEY
              I'm sorry if I got you into
              trouble. Maybe we don't have to,
              you know...unless you really want
              to.

                    WENDY
              Yeah.

                    MIKE
              I'm going to Silver Meadow, check
              out the ice storm...You wanna
              come?

                    WENDY
              Maybe. I don't know.

                    MIKE
              Yeah. OK. If you're there, I'll
              look for you.

INT. CARVER HOUSE. NIGHT.   139

Mikey, bundled up in a huge orange ski parka and cap, heads for
the door.

Sandy is watching Time Tunnel on the TV.

                              (CONTINUED)

CONTINUED: 139

                          SANDY
                Where you going?

                          MIKEY
                Out.

                          SANDY
                It's freezing.

                          MIKEY
                     (pausing)
                Yeah.

                          SANDY
                Then why you going out?

                          MIKEY
                     (thinking)
                When it freezes, I guess that
                means the molecules are not
                moving. So when you breathe,
                there's nothing in the air, you
                know, to breathe in to your body.
                The molecules have stopped. It's
                clean.

Sandy just looks at him. He walks out into the night.

INT. HALFORD HOUSE. NIGHT.   140

Elena sits on a couch, talking to no one, barely looking up,
when someone stands in front of her.

                          ELENA
                Reverend Edwards.

                          PHILIP
                Perhaps you might find it in your
                heart to call me Philip?

He sits beside her.

                          ELENA
                You're here...I'm a bit surprised.

                          PHILIP
                Sometimes the shepherd needs the
                company of the sheep.

                              (CONTINUED)

CONTINUED: 140

>   ELENA
>   I'm going to try hard <u>not</u> to
>   understand the implications of
>   that simile.

Philip's about to reply, but thinks better of it.

They sit glumly next to each other for a minute. Then Philip
rises.

>   PHILIP
>   Forgive me.

>   ELENA
>   Philip?

He walks swiftly to the hall and hurriedly fishes his keys out
of the bowl, then heads for the door. Elena has gotten up to
follow him.

>   TED FRANKLIN
>   (passing by)
>   I hope those weren't <u>my</u> keys.

He laughs at his own joke as Philip rushes out the front door.
Elena watches him go, even more forlorn than before.

INT. LIBBETS' BATHROOM. NIGHT.   141

Paul enters the bathroom. We hear Francis' and Libbets' voices
from the other room, laughing.

He pees.

At the sink, he pauses in front of the medicine cabinet, then
opens it.

>   PAUL
>   Eureka.

He pulls out some bottles.

>   PAUL
>   Valium. Seconal. Uh,
>   (can't quite pronounce
>   this one)
>   Par-er-goric?
>   (more)

                                        (CONTINUED)

CONTINUED: 141

> PAUL (Cont'd)
> (a beat, looking into
> the mirror for effect
> while holding up the
> Seconal)
> Francis Davenport the Fourth --
> tonight you sleep the sleep of the
> just.

He pockets the Seconal and turns out the light.

INT. LIBBETS' DEN. NIGHT.   142

Paul re-enters the den to find Francis alone.

> PAUL
> And whence has yon virginal maiden
> absconded?

> FRANCIS
> Like into one of the other 20 or
> so bathrooms they've got in this
> place.

Paul takes out the bottle and opens it.

> PAUL
> Check it out. Not for the faint
> of heart.

> FRANCIS
> Pharmaceutical! You are a god.

> PAUL
> (picking up beer,
> trying to hurry before
> Libbets returns)
> One for you and one for me.

He hands a pill to Francis, then pretends to pop one into his
mouth and takes a swig of his beer. As Francis downs his own,
Paul pockets his unswallowed pill.

> LIBBETS
> (in the doorway)
> No candy for me?

(CONTINUED)

                      FRANCIS
Groovy.
          (to Paul)
Young master of the revels, a
treat for our hostess?

                      PAUL
Well, uh, I don't, it's really --

                      LIBBETS
What is it?

                      FRANCIS
Come on Paulie, share the wealth.
You copped 'em from her mom's
stash anyway.

                      LIBBETS
Let's see!

                      PAUL
          (hand in pocket)
Libbets, you really shouldn't mix
and match, you know with the beer.
I'll put 'em back.

Libbets reaches into his pocket and pulls out the bottle.

                      LIBBETS
Oh far out, Paulie. Hey look,
these expired like five months
ago. You think they're better
aged?

She opens up the bottle and takes one out.

                      PAUL
Maybe you should have just a half.

                      LIBBETS
Thanks for the advice, Dad.

She takes the pill.

Paul looks on, thwarted.

INT. HALFORD HOUSE. NIGHT.   143

Ben is back at the bar, pouring another tall one. Mark Boland
sidles up next to him.

CONTINUED: 143

                       BOLAND
          Benjie, feeling no pain.

                       BEN
          As the Indian saying goes, pain is
          merely an opinion.

                       BOLAND
                (nodding across the
                room)
          Hey -- check it out. Maria
          Conrad's brought her son.
                (walking off)
          I wish some of the gang had
          brought their daughters!

Ben feels a wave of distaste at the joke.

He looks across the room as Maria and her son Neil (18, stringy
hair, acne, tie-dyed turtleneck, patched jeans) are engaging
Janey in conversation.

INT. LIBBETS' LIVING ROOM. NIGHT.   144

Paul, Francis, and Libbets sit on the floor, listening to the
music blasting at full strength.

Libbets and Francis are obviously on the verge of
unconsciousness. Paul regards them with a look of apprehension
on his face.

INT. HALFORD HOUSE. NIGHT.   145

Neil has now cornered Janey.

                       NEIL
          As Werner says, there is nothing
          to get. That's *It*. When you get
          that there's nothing to get.
          That's the training, when you ask
          yourself, the question, "What is
          is?"

                       JANEY
          Wait, this is the training, where
          they don't let you go to the
          bathroom?

                       (CONTINUED)

>   NEIL
> That was the hardest part. But I
> did it. And you get into some
> far-out shit.

INT. LIBBETS' LIVING ROOM. NIGHT.   146

Libbets puts a blanket over a sleeping Francis, who's crashed
out on the floor in a corner. Francis alternates between snores
and various mumbled delirious ravings.

>   FRANCIS
> The foot...the foot...toe clipper
> man...

Paul is sitting on the couch, and Libbets comes back and sits at
his feet, facing up to him.

>   PAUL
> I guess he's just real exhausted
> from, you know, tests and stuff.

Libbets is herself somewhat in dreamland.

>   LIBBETS
> Yeah.

>   PAUL
> You know Libbets, I really feel,
> you know, like a real connection
> to you --

>   LIBBETS
> Yeah but you don't even know me
> really.

>   PAUL
> Sure I do, you know, like your
> aura. That you give off.

>   LIBBETS
> My what?

>   PAUL
> It's like very positive, and I
> feel a real special feeling,
> because you really --

>   LIBBETS
> And I have a special feeling too,
> because I do. It's special.

(CONTINUED)

CONTINUED: 146

                    PAUL
          You do? I'm glad. Because I feel
          for you --

                    LIBBETS
          And I have a feeling for you too,
          because to me you're just like a--
          I feel for you like you're my own
          -- you're just like a--

                    PAUL AND LIBBETS
                  (simultaneously)
          -- a brother.

                    PAUL
          Yeah, you're not alone with that
          line.

                    LIBBETS
          I do. You are.

                    PAUL
          Right. Cool. So, how about we
          take a bath together?

                    LIBBETS
                  (consciousness fading
                   fast)
          Hah, hah, you're funny. A bath.
          Like a brother and sister. Oh
          man, I'm so wasted.

Her head bobs and weaves, her eyes close, and suddenly her head
falls forward with a whoosh toward the couch -- smack dab
between Paul's legs.

She begins to snore instantly, her open mouth nuzzling into his
crotch.

Paul doesn't move, doesn't even breathe. Then, slowly, he leans
his back into the couch, without shifting the rest of his body.

He looks as though he has simultaneously won the lottery and
received a lobotomy.

INT. HALFORD HOUSE. NIGHT.   147

The crowd's a bit thinner than before.

As Dot Halford begins calling out for everyone's attention, a
few couples make their embarrassed, last-minute way to the door.

                                              (CONTINUED)

>   DOT
> OK everyone. We have a little
> business to attend to now. So
> everyone who'd like to stay,
> please gather in the living room.

She scoops up the bowl and places it on a high end table which
has been put in the middle of the room.

There's an air of abject nervousness, as some couples leave,
some fake-happily put their arms around each other, and still
others circle, alone, slightly perspiring.

>   BEN
>   (walking up to Elena)
> Ready to go?

>   ELENA
> We're not going anywhere.

Elena waves at Janey Carver, who is standing across the living
room.

Janey looks back, without expression.

INT. LIBBETS' APARTMENT. NIGHT.   148

Libbets and Paul in the same position whence last we saw them.

Paul delicately leans to one side of the couch and picks up a
phone. He dials a number.

>   INTERCUT:

INT. HOOD LIVING ROOM. NIGHT.   149

The phone rings. Wendy picks it up.

>   WENDY
> Hood residence.

>   PAUL
>   (whispering)
> Charles?

>   WENDY
> Charles?

>   PAUL
> It is I.

                                        (CONTINUED)

94.

CONTINUED: 149

                        WENDY
          Isn't it like time for your train?

                        PAUL
          That's, um, why I was calling.
          I'm, uh, in the midst of a moral
          dilemma. And I was wondering,
          because I know you're a very moral
          person, and --

                        WENDY
          And?

Libbets moans and pushes her open mouth even further into his
lap.

                        PAUL
          Shit, Charles. I can't really
          talk about it right now. I guess
          I better get to the train.

                        WENDY
          Whatever.

Paul hangs up the phone and looks down at Libbets.

Libbets' Allman Brothers tape has run out. The machine makes a
repeated clicking sound as the take up reel continues to circle.
The only other sound is the noise of the wind and rain lashing
against the apartment's windows.

EXT. HOOD HOUSE. NIGHT.   150

Wendy emerges from the house and gets on her bike, but the ice
makes it too slippery. The storm is now in full swing. She
gets off, lets the bike fall to the ground, and walks.

EXT. STREET. NIGHT.   151

Wendy walks, barely keeping her balance in the wind. She pauses
at the same lonely corner where Mikey had earlier stopped and
had his brief epiphany.

She shivers, feeling the same cold breath that had touched him a
few days before.

INT. HALFORD HOUSE. NIGHT.   152

All the couples are now gathered for the key selection process,
men on one side of the room, women on the other. The storm can
be heard outside.

                    DOT
          Well, what shall the order be,
          alphabetical? In order of
          appearance?

                    PIERCE SAWYER
          Golf handicap! Lowest handicap
          does the honors.

Nervous laughter.

                    DOT
          Golf handicap? Ladies, isn't it
          up to you?

                    MARIA CONRAD
          Oh I'll go first, damn it. Let's
          just line up and get it over with.

Maria chooses Stephen Earle. Hands the keys to him. A
smattering of applause as she takes his arm and they leave.

                    MARIE EARLE
          Good luck!

Neil watches his mother's exit.

                    JUMP CUT TO:

A few more couplings.

                    JUMP CUT TO:

Helen Worthington approaches the bowl. Helen Worthington has
the size and shape of a sumo wrestler.

There is a nervous shifting of weight on the male side of the
room.

Helen delicately reaches into the bowl. Her hands emerge with a
key chain.

George Clair steps forward, obviously depressed, as a collective
sigh of relief goes up from behind him. Ben looks on,
momentarily triumphant.

                    (CONTINUED)

CONTINUED: 152

Elena smiles to herself.

                                        JUMP CUT TO:

The Gadds choose each other.

                         MRS. GADD
                    Oh, my own husband. Isn't that
                    against the rules?

                         DOT
                    Try again?

                         MRS. GADD
                         (relieved)
                    Oh, I think not.

Mr.Gadd smiles as they leave, obviously happy to go.

Finally, only Mark Boland, Neil Conrad, Janey and Jim Carver,
Rob and Dot Halford, Sari Steele, Benjamin and Elena.

                         DOT
                    Getting down to the wire!

Janey steps forward. Benjamin is obviously agitated.

Close on Janey's hands selecting -- away from Ben's equine key
ring.

She lifts up another key ring -- Neil Conrad, the teenager.

She hands the self-important-looking Neil his keys and they turn
to go.

Jim Carver smiles mysteriously to himself.

Ben suddenly lurches forward, semi-drunkenly, trying to separate
Neil from Janey.

                         THE GROUP
                         (ad lib)
                    Hey, hey, Ben, hang on there a
                    sec.

He backs off, ashamed, and, taking a step backwards, trips over
the coffee table.

Mark Boland helps lift him up.

                         BEN
                    Sorry...maybe I should...the
                    bathroom?

                                        (CONTINUED)

CONTINUED: (2)   152

                         DOT
          Right down the hall, Ben.

                         BEN
               (muttering)
          Sorry, I'm sorry. Uh, I'll be
          back.

Dot follows Mark Boland down the hall behind Ben.

Suddenly, it's just Elena and Jim Carver, and Sari Steele and
Rob Halford.

                         ROB HALFORD
               (taking Sari's arm)
          Actually, we didn't put our keys
          in at all. But you won't spread
          it around? It's my party, and Dot
          isn't... hey, we're just going to
          slip upstairs for a while. You
          folks like a cup of coffee or
          something before we go?

Elena and Jim look at each other.

                         ELENA
          Rob, we'll fix it for ourselves.
          You two go and get acquainted.
          We'll let ourselves out the front
          door.

Jim and Elena stand there alone.

                         JIM
          Well, I have to say I don't have
          much faith that my car keys are
          still in that bowl. Doesn't seem
          entirely safe, leaving your car
          keys around?

                         ELENA
          Let me.

She takes the bowl and dips her hand in. Two sets are left.
One, her own, she avoids. She takes out Jim's keys and walks
across the room, handing them to him.

                         JIM
          Thanks, but -- oh, I don't think
          so. It's been kind of a
          discouraging evening.

                                        (CONTINUED)

CONTINUED: (3)   152

                    ELENA
          You couldn't have hoped for much
          better when you came up the walk.

                    JIM
          Somehow it was different in my
          imagination when I thought about
          it. Actually, I didn't think
          about it at all, really.

They sit down on the sofa.

                    JIM
          You want coffee or something?

                    ELENA
          Well, maybe they have one of those
          filter jobs in the kitchen --

                    JIM
          Look, Elena, the fact that we're
          neighbors...you know, close
          friends, well it sort of makes
          this a little strange, don't you
          think?

                    ELENA
          My husband is probably passed out
          in the bathroom, or at least he
          wishes he were. I've been married
          to him for 17 years and I don't
          have any intention of going in
          there to get him... So what I'm
          proposing is that since your wife
          has gone off with a boy, and since
          you are standing here alone, I'm
          proposing that you and I do what
          makes sense. Stay warm. Pass
          some time. That's all.

They both look at their hands.

                    ELENA
          Now don't make me feel as if I'm
          being too forward, OK? If you
          don't --

                    JIM
          What the hey. Let's go for a
          drive.

                                        (CONTINUED)

CONTINUED: (4)   152

> ELENA
> Okay. Shall we clean up around
> here first? Do you think it's all
> right --

> JIM
> Nah, that wasn't in the contract.

But they still walk around turning off lights.

In the hallway, Elena looks a bit mournfully at the light
seeping from underneath the bathroom door. She hears the sound
of running water from inside.

Then she goes into a sideroom and joins Jim. They pick up their
coats.

EXT. HALFORD HOUSE. NIGHT.   153

Elena and Jim walk outside into the freezing, pelting rain.

Covering their faces, they jog to his car, an oversized
Cadillac. A thick glaze of ice forms on his windshield.

INT. JIM'S CADILLAC. NIGHT.   154

They climb in.

> JIM
> We're going to have to defrost
> this thing for a while.

He turns on the ignition, and the vents start to blow cold air
at them.

He leans over and kisses her.

> ELENA
> Do these seats go back?

That starts it. He jumps at her, unbuckling her and unzipping
himself.

They tangle uncomfortably for a few seconds. And then,
comically, he's in her.

With a groan, it's over in a flash.

Jim pulls himself off, readjusting his pants.

(CONTINUED)

CONTINUED: 154

> JIM
> That was awful, really awful. I'm
> so sorry, Elena.

Elena has somehow worked herself into the cavity of the glove
compartment, and is trying to figure out how to extricate
herself.

> JIM
> Things are really rotten at home.
> You wouldn't believe how rotten.
> Janey's sick. She's unstable, I
> guess. . .it's not the right time
> to tell you. . .but that's it --
> it's like I can't make her happy,
> the boys can't make her happy, she
> just doesn't ---

> ELENA
> Jim, maybe we should just go.
> I've got to look in on the kids.
> Paul is supposed to be coming back
> in from the city.

> JIM
> Jesus, let me make it up to you --
> I can do better than that,
> honestly --

> ELENA
> Well, we can talk about it.

> JIM
> That's fine. I wouldn't expect
> you to see it any other way.

> ELENA
> Maybe you just need -- look, can
> you wait here a sec, I need to
> tidy up -- just a minute, I'll be
> right back. You'll wait?

> JIM
> Of course.

She opens the door and walks back to the house.

INT. HALFORD HOUSE. NIGHT.   155

Elena hesitantly walks to the bathroom.

                                        (CONTINUED)

She opens the door. Ben's sitting on the floor, next to the
toilet, woozily flipping through the pages of a magazine.

> BEN
>
> Elena.

> ELENA
>
> Ben, I've got a ride home. Maybe
> you should sleep this one off on
> the couch here?

> BEN
>
> I'll drive you --

> ELENA
>
> Ben.

She sits on the toilet next to him, stroking his hair.

> ELENA
>
> You're in no condition to drive.
> We'll talk in the morning, OK?

He sits, accepting and quiet.

> ELENA
>
> You'll get some sleep on the couch
> out there?

> BEN
> (looking up at her,
> with gratitude)
> Sure. I'll try. And we'll talk
> in the morning?

> ELENA
>
> We'll talk in the morning.

EXT. CARVER HOUSE. NIGHT.   156

Wendy walks up the drive in the rain, pauses, then goes to the
front door and knocks lightly. The door swings ajar. She
pushes on it, and lets herself in.

INT. CARVER HOUSE. NIGHT.   157

> WENDY
>
> Anyone home? Hello.

(CONTINUED)

Wendy wanders into the living room, then climbs the steps. The
sound of the wind and the darkness begin to scare her.

She goes into Mikey's room -- it's even more of a disaster zone
than usual.

She sees on the wall his dark-light poster of the 12 (sexual)
positions of the zodiac.

She notices the black garter belt on the floor, and picks it up,
absent-mindedly swinging it in her hand as she walks out of the
room.

She walks back down the stairs and into the kitchen, leaving the
garter belt on the counter.

She opens the refrigerator, grabs a jar of peanut butter, and
scoops some up in her finger. As she puts her finger in her
mouth --

                    SANDY
          Wendy.

She gives out a little yelp.

                    WENDY
          Sandy, you scared the shit out of
          me.

                    SANDY
          What are you doing?

                    WENDY
          Just thought I'd stop by.

                    SANDY
          Mike's out -- I think he went to
          Silver Meadow to see if you were
          hanging around there.

                    WENDY
          Yeah.

                    SANDY
               (pause)
          Are you his girlfriend?

                    WENDY
          No.

INT. JIM'S CADILLAC. NIGHT.   158

Elena gets in. They drive off silently.

EXT. STREETS. NIGHT.   159

The car moves haltingly through the sleet and ice, inches up a
hill, then falters and slides back silently, circling a couple
of times before crashing into an embankment.

INT. JIM'S CADILLAC. NIGHT.   160

As the car slides and crashes amid Jim's and Elena's screams.

Silence.

                    JIM
          You okay?

                         ELENA
          Yeah. You?

                    JIM
          Yes. Well, I guess we can walk
          from here.

EXT. JIM'S CADILLAC. NIGHT.   161

Jim and Elena get out, shaky, from the car.

They pause for a moment.

The street lamp above them sizzles, but stays on.

They start to walk.

INT. LIBBETS' LIVING ROOM. NIGHT.   162

Paul and Libbets, still frozen in the same position. Finally,
Paul gently pushes Libbets' head back.

It slides off his leg and, as Paul lurches forward in a failed
attempt to grab it, Libbets flops backwards, her head hitting
the carpet with a dull but decidedly loud thump.

                    PAUL
          Oh, shit!

Paul gets up, looks down at her.

                                                  (CONTINUED)

CONTINUED: 162

She snores.

He runs over to a side table and sees the clock: 11:10.

                    PAUL
          Oh shit oh shit.

He grabs his comic books and runs for the door.

INT. TAXI. NIGHT.   163

The driver impassively inches down Park Avenue.

                    PAUL
          Oh shit oh shit.

INT. TRAIN. NIGHT.   164

Paul sprints into the train just as the doors are closing.

INT. TRAIN. NIGHT   165

Paul walks through the nearly empty train car and finds a seat.
He pulls his *Fantastic Four* comic book out of his coat pocket.

INT. HALFORD LIVING ROOM. NIGHT.   166

Ben makes his way into the living room and heads for the front
door. He pauses for a moment, smiles, and heads back for the
living room.

He goes to the bowl, and with a look of dawning self-
consciousness and a brief chuckle, pulls his keys out -- the
last set.

INT. SANDY'S ROOM. NIGHT.   167

Sandy and Wendy are sitting on the floor. He grabs his G.I.
Joe.

                    SANDY
          Check this out. He's supposed to
          talk all kinds of stuff, but he's
          like malfunctioned.

He pulls the dog tag on the doll, and G.I. Joe emits a plastic
macho voice.

                                              (CONTINUED)

CONTINUED: 167

>   G.I. JOE
>   Mayday! Mayday! Get this message
>   back to base!
>
>   SANDY
>   Same thing. Again and again.

Wendy takes the doll and yanks the cord.

>   G.I. JOE
>   Mayday! Mayday! Get this message
>   back to base!
>
>   SANDY
>   It's gonna get a lot colder
>   tonight, I predict. Probably a
>   blackout. Do you have candles in
>   your house? I know where the
>   candles are, and I have my own
>   flashlight. Over there. Also, I
>   know where every emergency exit is
>   on this floor.

During the course of his monologue, as Wendy looks on, Sandy
calmly ties a noose for his doll.

>   SANDY
>   This knot's called a bowline.

He puts the noose over the doll's head, as Wendy holds the doll
for him.

>   G.I. JOE
>   Mayday! Mayday!
>
>   SANDY
>   Let's hang him.

Sandy drapes the noose over the edge of a dresser drawer. G.I.
Joe dangles. They both look at him in silence.

The silence continues.

>   WENDY
>   He's dead.
>
>   SANDY
>   If it wasn't raining we could take
>   him outside and blow him up.

                                        (CONTINUED)

CONTINUED: (2)   167

> WENDY
> He wouldn't blow up. He'd just
> get all mangled or twisted.

She takes the doll down and lays him flat on the bed. And then
begins to remove its clothes.

Sandy looks on, desirous.

> WENDY
> Well.
>   (noticing his lack of
>   anatomy)
> It looks like someone got to his
> private parts before us.

> SANDY
> Communist Viet Cong.

> WENDY
> They left it in the jungle.

They speak with high seriousness.

Wendy slides up on the bed where Sandy sits, a pillow on his
lap, and one by one, with exaggerated slowness, she removes her
snowboots as if they were stiletto heels.

> WENDY
> Can I get into your bed?
>   (pause)
> With you?

Sandy begins to shake.

> SANDY
> We -- we have to go to the guest
> room. We can't stay in here.
> What if Mikey? My parents?

> WENDY
> Don't worry about them. They're
> at that party, getting drunk and
> falling all over each other and
> making jokes about McGovern and
> stuff.

Sandy begins to cry.

> SANDY
> It's just -- it's just --

(CONTINUED)

CONTINUED: (3)   167

She takes his hand, and they walk out of the room and down the
hall, into the guest room.

INT. GUEST ROOM. NIGHT.   168

Wendy and Sandy enter. She sees the vodka bottle on the
dresser.

                    WENDY
          Want a drink?

                    SANDY
          Vodka?

                    WENDY
          You never tasted the stuff?

She fills the glass to the brim and hands the bottle to Sandy.

They clink and each toss back a sip.

Sandy coughs and gags, but swallows.

                    WENDY
          Try again.

He does.

                    SANDY
          It feels warm.

                    WENDY
          One more shot?

                    SANDY
          Okay.

They drink.

                    WENDY
          Under the covers.

Under they go, and soon every layer of clothing emerges.

                    WENDY
             (feeling her way)
          Get 'em off.

Sandy begins to laugh, and soon Wendy joins him.

They roll around on top of each other for a while.

                                        (CONTINUED)

CONTINUED:

> WENDY
> Have you ever had a nocturnal
> emission?

> SANDY
> Huh?

> WENDY
> That's the name for when you wake
> up and find this little pool of
> sticky stuff, like after a sexy
> dream.

Sandy shakes his head.

> WENDY
> They didn't tell you this stuff
> yet? What planet do you live on?

Sandy doesn't answer, but climbs back on top of her and kisses
her neck.

> SANDY
> I love you.

> WENDY
> That's nice. Are you drunk?

> SANDY
> I don't know. How do I know?

> WENDY
> I don't know either. You spin
> around, when you lie down.

Sandy rolls off her and lies on his back.

> SANDY
> I don't think I'm spinning.

They cuddle up together.

He yawns. She yawns.

EXT. SILVER MEADOW. NIGHT.

Mikey walks along the edge of the empty pool in the rain. He
climbs up on the diving board and bounces lightly on it, but
then gets off and stands, looking down at the pool again.

EXT. SILVER MEADOW. NIGHT.   170

Mikey walks across the field. The rain is pretty much over.

EXT. STREET. NIGHT.   171

An odd stillness. The storm has let up, leaving icicles forming
on the tree branches and fence posts. Mikey walks along. With
a running start, he slides on the ice.

He walks back up and slides again, hollering with joy. He is an
image of a tiny yet absolute and positive freedom.

The streetlights sputter on, then off.

INT. CARVER GUEST ROOM. NIGHT.   172

Sandy and Wendy lie asleep.

EXT. STREET. NIGHT.   173

The same corner where previously Mikey, and later Wendy, paused.

A power line is down. It hisses and HUMS -- a humming very much
like the humming Mikey has been hearing earlier.

The humming takes on the same transcendent tonality to which
Mikey has become so accustomed at such moments.

Mikey sits down on a metal street guardrail, to ponder the sound
and the snaking coil of electricity.

A strange look of almost religious wonder overcomes his face, as
the power line connects to the guardrail.

                    MIKEY
          Oh, shit.

Glued by an electrical pulse to the rail, he shakes as the
current flows through him.

After a minute, his body slumps and slides down the road.

INT. TRAIN. NIGHT.   174

As Paul sits reading on the moving train, the lights inside
begin to sputter, and the train begins to slow.

                              (CONTINUED)

CONTINUED: 174

After a few moments, the train grinds to a halt, and Paul and
his few fellow late-night passengers are left in near total
dark, with only the light of an emergency exit sign above Paul's
head to light the scene.

The train is eerily silent.

EXT. HOOD CAR. NIGHT. 175

Ben drives home.

EXT. STREET IN FRONT OF CARVER HOUSE. PRE-DAWN. 176

Jim and Elena arrive on foot.

                    JIM
          You want to come in, get a cup of
          coffee -- warm up? I can either
          walk you home, or you could crash
          in the guest room.

                    ELENA
          Sure. Maybe coffee. Then a walk
          home.

She takes off her soaking wet shoes as she enters the house.

INT. CARVER KITCHEN. PRE-DAWN. 177

                    JIM
               (hanging up the phone)
          Phone's out. I hope the pipe's --
          ah --

He walks into the kitchen. The pipes have begun to burst.
There's a water leak running down the walls, forming a puddle on
the floor.

Elena has walked into the kitchen behind him. She leans against
the counter, picking up the garter belt without thinking for a
second, then putting it back down.

                    JIM
          Oh, well. Why don't you put on
          some dry socks -- and we've got
          some rain boots in the guest
          closet back there. Last room
          upstairs -- back of the hall.

                                        (CONTINUED)

CONTINUED: 177

Elena climbs the stairs in her bare feet.

INT. CARVER GUEST ROOM. CONT'D.   178

Elena opens the door, and discovers Wendy and Sandy asleep. She
stands before the bed, and gazes down on them.

They look almost angelic.

Wendy, sensing her presence in the room, opens her eyes, slowly
coming out of sleep.

                    ELENA
             (heartbroken, softly)
        Get dressed.

Elena walks out of the room, back to the kitchen.

Wendy gets out of bed quietly, leaving Sandy sleeping
peacefully.

She looks at him lovingly, and tucks the blanket back up around
him.

INT. CARVER KITCHEN. PRE-DAWN.   179

Elena and Jim are drinking coffee.

                    ELENA
        You should let him sleep.

Wendy enters. She looks inquisitively at the two adults.

                    WENDY
        Where's Dad?

INT. HOOD CAR. PRE-DAWN.   180

Ben continues to drive slowly. He looks out his side window,
and sees something -- the glow of an orange parka. He puts on
his brakes.

EXT. STREET. PRE-DAWN.   181

Ben gets out of the car, and stands on the top of an icy
embankment. In a clump of bushes is Mikey's body.

                        (CONTINUED)

CONTINUED: 181

He walks hesitantly toward it. Mike's body lies face down in
the wet slush.

Ben leans down and turns the body over, then stands back in
amazement and saddened shock.

He bends over the body, and tries a cursory, futile mouth-to-
mouth.

He stands back up for a moment, then picks Mike's body up,
carrying him over the hill and onto the street. We see now that
he is parked just a short block from the Carver's house.

He bypasses his car and walks directly down the street toward
the house. The effort is obviously enormous. He falls from
time to time, then gets back up.

INT. TRAIN. PRE-DAWN.   182

Various passengers asleep.

Paul, hunched up in his seat under the faint emergency exit
light, cold. He reads his comic book by the light of the
emergency exit.

                    "DON'T YOU SEE, SUE? HE WAS TOO
                    POWERFUL...IF HIS ENERGY HAD
                    CONTINUED TO BUILD, HE WOULD HAVE
                    DESTROYED THE WORLD!"

Suddenly, the lights begin to flicker on and the hum of the
train's engines returns.

The conductor enters the car, blasting forth in his classic
nasal train conductor voice.

                    CONDUCTOR
              Good morning ladies and
              gentlemen --

On Paul, squinting in the harsh light. We are back at the
flashforward from the beginning of the film.

EXT. TRAIN BRIDGE. PRE-DAWN.   183

The train moves slowly through a suburban, semi-forested
landscape. On the street below the bridge, an emergency highway
crew is removing a fallen tree, their trucks aglow in flashing
yellow lights.

INT. CARVER KITCHEN. DAWN.   184

Elena pours Wendy a cup of coffee. They're both in their coats.

                    WENDY
          I don't like coffee.

                    ELENA
          It'll warm you up.

Elena sits next to her. They both cross their legs, then raise
their cups and sip the coffee, not noticing the simultaneity of
their movements.

INT. GUEST ROOM. DAWN.   185

Jim watches the sleeping Sandy, picks up the half-empty bottle
of vodka, pours himself a drink. The noise wakes Sandy up. Jim
sits down on the bed at his feet.

                    SANDY
          Dad?

                    JIM
          Sandy.

Jim raises a quiet toast to his son and takes a gulp of vodka.

INT. KITCHEN. DAWN.   186

Elena and Wendy hear a hollering from outside, get up to see
what it is.

EXT. CARVER HOUSE. DAWN.   187

Elena and Wendy come out the front door, as Ben lays Mikey's
body onto the ground before the front steps.

                    ELENA
          Ben?

He's too breathless to speak.

They stand there, looking down at Mikey.

Behind Elena and Wendy, Jim appears.

He pushes softly by them toward the body of his son.

                              (CONTINUED)

CONTINUED: 187

                    BEN
          Jim -- he was just up -- in
          Silver Lane -- I think maybe -- a
          power line --

Jim picks up his son.

He carries him silently into the house.

Sandy, now standing inside the foyer, pushes himself back
against the wall as they pass, without expression.

After a moment, from outside, the Hoods can hear Jim's wailing.

                    BEN
          Do you think? Maybe we should
          call someone --

                    ELENA
          The phone's out.

                    BEN
          Yeah. Well, we can just --

                    ELENA
          Ben, I don't know if he really
          wants us here.

Wendy has been watching Sandy through the screen door.

                    WENDY
          Wait, I --

She turns back up the front steps and gently goes in --

INT. CARVER LIVING ROOM. CONT'D.   188

On the living room floor, Jim is hugging Mike's body, his
shoulders shaking uncontrollably, sobbing.

Wendy walks and stands next to Sandy, who is filled momentarily
with a brief inexplicable rush of anger toward her -- but she
takes him and gives him an awkward, childlike hug, then turns
and runs out the door, joining Ben and Elena on the driveway.
Sandy watches her go, his face wet with tears.

EXT. CARVER HOUSE. CONT'D.   189

                    ELENA
          Oh, you know, for a minute I
          thought it was --

                    BEN
          Paul? Yeah. You think --

                    WENDY
          He's probably been waiting all
          night at the station.

                    BEN
          C'mon.

EXT. STREET. DAWN.   190

Elena, Wendy, and Ben reach the car and get in. The car starts
and drives off.

There are now crews out cleaning up the storm's debris and
fixing the power lines as they drive.

INT. HOOD'S CAR. DAWN.   191

Wendy is in the back seat. As Ben drives, Elena looks over to
him. He catches her eye. They both turn their gazes back to
the road. But then, as if on cue, they look again at each
other.

Briefly, but deeply, they look and see each other.

EXT. CONRAIL STATION. EARLY MORNING.   192

The train slowly pulls in. The Hood family walks down to the
end of the platform.

The train doors open, and Paul, tired and a bit cramped,
emerges. He sees his family gathered at the other end of the
platform, and walks to them.

They stand, silent, even dignified, awaiting him.

When he joins them they all walk silently to the car and get in.

INT. HOOD CAR. EARLY MORNING.   193

Sunlight floods in and temporarily blinds Ben as he starts the
engine.

                                        (CONTINUED)

CONTINUED: 193

He squints, his eyes tearing a bit from the light.

He looks around, first at his wife, then at his two children sitting in the back seat.

He turns off the engine. Quietly, he begins to cry.

He turns to the back seat and smiles, crying, at his children.

                    ELENA
                (softly)
          Ben.

Paul looks at Wendy, silently asking her what's happening.

She casts her eyes downward, as does he.

                    ELENA
                (her hand still not yet
                 touching him)
          Ben.

EXT. STATION PARKING LOT. MORNING.   194

From above:

The car, the first morning light shining upon it.

STILLS

Above: "Gotcha." Producer Ted Hope with Joan Allen and Kevin Kline.

WENDY
Christina Ricci

JANEY
Sigourney Weaver

SANDY
Adam Hann-Byrd

PAUL
Tobey Maguire

BEN
Kevin Kline

ELENA
Joan Allen

JIM
Jamey Sheridan

MIKEY
Elijah Wood

Above: "Into the void." Paul *(Tobey Maguire)* finds his family at the train station.
Below: "Anti-matter." Preparing the final scene at the New Canaan train station, the art department applies plastic icicles and the effects team's famous "splooge" under a sweltering sun: the thermometer hit eighty-five degrees during the shooting of the scene.

Above: "We actually enjoy it." Ben *(Kevin Kline)* offers the phone to Wendy *(Christina Ricci)*.
Below: "Think of the money supply as a large male organ." Ben *(Kline)* philosophizes on
   the job.

Above: "Breaking down the old Unitarian barriers." The Reverend Edwards *(Michael Cumpsty)* talks shop with Elena *(Joan Allen).*
Below: "You look very—free." Wendy *(Ricci)* testing the limits.

Above: "Your needs. My needs." Janey *(Sigourney Weaver)* and Ben *(Kline)* in the guest room.

Above: "We've got to trade this thing in for a normal bed." Jim *(Jamey Sheridan)* returns
home to Janey *(Weaver)*.
Below: "Going in all the way." Janey *(Weaver)* ducks for cover.

Above: "They were old. And they couldn't fly anyway." Sandy *(Adam Hann-Byrd)* at play.

Above: "Play with the whip." Janey *(Weaver)* in a maternal moment.

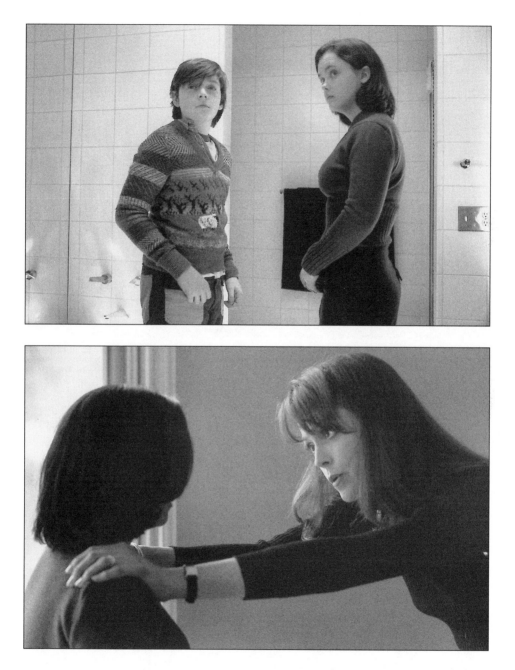

Above: "I'll show you mine if you show me yours." Wendy *(Ricci)* initiates Sandy *(Hann-Byrd)*.
Below: "In Samoa and in other developing nations." Janey *(Weaver)* lectures Wendy *(Ricci)* on
the facts of life.

Above: "It's a one-on-one kind of date thing." Paul *(Maguire)* borrows Wendy's phone.
Below: "You used to love to say grace, remember?" Thanksgiving at the Hood house.

Above: "Even the invisible girl becomes visible." Ang Lee directs Joan Allen.

Below: "Birth control." Ben *(Kline)* does some imaginary golfing in his boxer shorts after Janey *(Weaver)* has ditched him.

Above: "I'll carry you." Wendy *(Ricci)* in her father's arms.
Below: "New this year." The key bowl is presented to a befuddled Ben and Elena *(Kline and Allen).*

Above: "Strictly volunteer, of course." The keys.
Below: "A prior engagement overcame me." Janey *(Weaver)* clears the air with Ben *(Kline)*.

Above: "Wait, this is the training, where they don't let you go to the bathroom?" Janey *(Weaver)* learns about EST from Neal *(Glenn Fitzpatrick)*.

Above: "We're not going anywhere." Ang Lee rehearses the key party with a nervous cast as James Schamus looks on.
Below: "Another shot?" Sandy *(Hann-Byrd)* and Wendy *(Ricci)* prepare for bedtime.

Above: "It's special." Libbets *(Katie Holmes)* attempts to understand her aura.
Below: "Isn't it up to us?" The key selection begins.

Above: "Do these seats go back?" Elena *(Allen)* and Jim *(Sheridan)* commence the briefest love scene in cinema history.

Above: "I don't think so." Elena *(Allen)* hands Jim *(Sheridan)* his car keys.
Below: "Oh, no." Cinematographer Fred Elmes and Ang Lee contemplate the final moments of Mikey *(Elijah Wood)*.

Above: "For a moment I thought it was…Paul." Waiting at the station.

SCENE NOTES

BY JAMES SCHAMUS

There are, of course, hundreds if not thousands of differences between screenplay and finished film. I will pass over in silence the vast majority of them and note only those that indicate the more important thematic and dramatic changes we made on the journey from script to screen.

Sc. 2–4: We simplified the voice-over as the combination of opening credits, comic-book images, text, music, and voice-over was simply too much information for anyone but Hal the computer to take in at the opening of a film.

Sc. 16: A mistake—Thai stick would have been purchased not by the bag, but by the stick.

Sc. 6–11: The entire therapy sequence was cut during production. This became part of a general movement away from the social satire and comedy in the script and toward a more focused dramatic structure.

Sc. 20–21: Much of the babble at the dinner party table was trimmed, mainly to pick up the pace of the sequence, as well as to ease up on the social satire.

Sc. 24: Omitted, mainly because we didn't have time to do an entire night exterior lighting setup solely for a few kisses good-bye.

Sc. 31–35: We decided to drop Janey and Ben's encounter on the train in order to give their affair a bit more of a history. It would have been a great comic scene for Sigourney and Kevin.... And the exquisite tragicomedy of Ben's "money supply as phallus" speech was also reluctantly cut during postproduction, along with his bantering with office rival George St. Clair, superbly performed by Henry Czerny, who can still be seen in the key party. Instead, well into the editing process, we realized that the early focus of the film had to remain rooted in New Canaan and in the more dramatic feelings of yearning and loss that were propelling the characters through the rest of the film. Ben's trip to work in New York was thus reconceived to be more of a melancholic interlude than a comedic sequence.

Sc. 36: The "humming" motif, which played prominently in the script as a kind of foreboding music of the spheres for which only Mikey's ears are available, was more or less removed by the final edit. Mikey's fate is foreshadowed strongly enough through Elijah Wood's performance—we didn't feel the need to prop it up with sound effects.

Sc. 54: We removed this scene from the final cut of the film—a scene Ang cherished as one of the best acted and edited he'd ever directed—simply because Elena and Philip's interactions worked so economically in their other two scenes. This one was sacrificed for reasons of pacing and focus. Michael Cumpsty's depiction of Philip's essentially genial and lonely soul, Joan Allen's near caress of his hand at the end of the scene, and Kate Burton's hilarious take on the town gossip made this certainly one of the most painful cuts from the film—it was a near perfect scene. And Ang had gotten an entire background through the coffee shop windows depicting a long line of cars waiting for gas—a nice image that gave us both a taste of the 1973 oil crisis and an emblem of the crisis of consumption afflicting the community.

Sc. 59-64: Shooting a film that takes place during Thanksgiving in the spring had its pleasures as well as its terrors, and these scenes counted among the latter. We were able to shoot the interior car dialogue between Janey and Elena, as well as Elena being dropped off in town and her initial bike riding, but location scheduling and a host of other production issues left us shy of the pickup itself, just as virtually every tree, bush, and flower in New Canaan decided to bloom. We pushed the scene to the end of the production schedule, hoping to find an alternative treeless location, but by the final week of shooting realized we could live without the sequence as a whole—the brief interaction between the two women at the Carvers' dinner party told enough of the story.

Sc. 94: The masturbation speech, which in an earlier draft of the script actually served as the opening of the film, was much reduced in the editing—again, part of an overall strategy to decrease the comedic side of the film in favor of the more familial. Note the moody music that now plays under this scene.

Sc. 99–102: We decided not to shoot the pot-smoking in the bathroom scene and to drop the sports poster scene in the editing room, in order to craft the Thanksgiving day celebration as less of a sequence than as a kind of beat—a brief moment before the final descent of the last act.

Sc. 128–173: The entire final night was rearranged many times in the editing room, with each story line interwoven with the others a number of different ways until we ended up with a final solution to the puzzle. We always expected this to be so, because what can appear on the page to be decisive and witty crosscutting can seem labored and unfocused on the screen. Ang was also able to create a large number of thematic and visual echoes from scene to scene during the shooting, many of which worked in combinations we could hardly have surmised until after we commenced the editing process. In the end, Ben's pot smoking, Paul's call home to Wendy, Wendy's blasé attempt at "suicide"—all of these were cut while the rest of the scenes, especially the key selection sequence, ended up getting scrambled and reordered. Mikey's final words were changed from "Oh, shit" back to the book's original "Oh, no." Rick Moody rightly pointed out to us that the original emphasized Mikey's wonder while the script made him out to be too much the worldly teenager.

Sc. 187–188: During rehearsals Sigourney asked us about the fate of her character and talked about how she would see Janey at the end of the film. Ang immediately seized on her suggestions, and powerfully so. We had never wanted to bring Janey back to the scene in the living room. As a film scene, it would have called for a melodramatic response that would have been impossible to stage without pathos, and we were worried that it might look as though we were punishing her character for her independence and rebellion, something we very much wanted to avoid. But to see Janey's eyes flutter open as she awakes at the sound of her husband's cries and, from there, to imagine the rest of her journey seemed a far more just resolution to her story than simply omitting her from the final moments of the film, and Ang came particularly to relish, too, her return to the quiet house and her pause in front of the boys' room. As she curls up into a fetal position on the water bed, an object of comic derision earlier in the film, the movement and sound of the water serve as a subtle contrast to the hardening ice of the storm outside.

Sc. 194: As the editing of the film progressed, we began to understand that, however it could be accounted for, something of the novel's first-person voice was also emerging from the film—that, after all, it was Paul's story we were finally telling, even if we had constructed the screenplay as an ensemble work. We realized that it was appropriate to hear Paul's voice again in the moments after Mikey's death, both to recuperate somewhat from the shock of the killing as well as to fold the emotional registers of that shock into one primary consciousness. The voice-over we came up with for Paul is neither a summary nor a celebration; it avoids the direct reference to the comic book even as it builds from the worldview his reading of the book has developed during the previous voice-overs:

PAUL

(voice-over)

```
When you think about it, it's not easy to keep from
just wandering out of life. It's like someone is
always leaving the door open to the next world,
and if you aren't paying attention, you could just
walk through it. And then you've died. That's
why sometimes in your dreams it's like you're
standing in that doorway and the dying people
and the newborn people pass you by and brush up
against you as they come in and out of the world
during the night. You get spun around, and in
the morning, it takes a while to find your way back
into the world.
```

At the end of the film, it is Paul's face on which we finally hold. It is his vision of his father's tears through which he and, we hope, the film as a whole achieves a troubled but still liberating epiphany, a kind of embarrassment of forgiveness.

Ang and his production team spent months researching every aspect of American life in the seventies, and as preproduction progressed Ang began to pull from the research the essential themes and emotions he hoped to organize the film around. With the assistance of researcher Jean Castelli, he even put together a theme chart for the crew, which helped identify where he saw patterns and echoes that might inform each creative department's work.

Scene	Time/Day	Weather	Themes	Echoes	Motifs	Warmth
27. INT. WENDY'S ROOM (*Wendy on the phone*)	NIGHT				Nixon	
28. INT. HOOD UPSTAIRS HALLWAY (*Elena and Ben come home*)	NIGHT			look down hall towards kitchen with Ben/ Elena, like in Sc. 57		
29. INT. WENDY'S ROOM (*Ben says goodnight to his daugther.*)	NIGHT		inconsistent dad behavior		Nixon	parental affection: Ben and Wendy
29A EXT. HOOD HOUSE	NIGHT				establishing	
Day 4 Mon. Nov. 19						
30. EXT. NEW CANAAN TRAIN STATION (*Men in gray flannel suits off to work, c.1973*)	DAY WITH SUN				advertising images; train/commuting; power lines	
31. INT. TRAIN	DAY WITH SUN		pushing the limits (boredom)	Ben spaces out like Paul	advertising images; train/commuting/sex; power lines	
32. MANHATTAN OFFICE BUILDING	DAY WITH SUN			tunnel tilt to sky line, like Paul at night		
33. SHACKLEY AND SCHWIMMER CONF RM (*Stagflation*)	DAY WITH SUN		looking for patterns (macroeconomic)	displaced desire/frustration (cf. "facts of life")	'73 zeitgeist; distraction (Ben); glass + reflection	
34. INT. BEN HOOD'S OFFICE (*George vs. Ben at work*)	DAY WITH SUN		peer pressure: redefining/opening up institutions: up the organization	like father like son: Paul/Francis-Ben/George; Ben + Elena looking for meaning of life	'73 zeitgeist; aggression (George)	

CAST AND CREW CREDITS

Fox Searchlight Presents
A Good Machine Production
An Ang Lee Film

Kevin Kline

THE ICE STORM

Joan Allen	Tobey Maguire
Henry Czerny	Christina Ricci
Adam Hann-Byrd	Jamey Sheridan
David Krumholtz	Elijah Wood

and Sigourney Weaver

Casting by
Avy Kaufman

Costume Designer
Carol Oditz

Associate Producers
Alysse Bezahler
Anthony Bregman

Composer
Mychael Danna

Based on the novel by
Rick Moody

Film Editor
Tim Squyres

Production Designer
Mark Friedberg

Director of Photography
Frederick Elmes, A.S.C.

Screenplay by
James Schamus

Produced by
Ted Hope
James Schamus
and Ang Lee

Directed by
Ang Lee

CAST

listed in alphabetical order

elena hood	Joan ALLEN	francis davenport	David KRUMHOLTZ
dorothy franklin	Kate BURTON	weatherman	Daniel McDONALD
ted shackley	William CAIN	paul hood	Tobey MAGUIRE
philip edwards	Michael CUMPSTY	mr. gadd	Miles MAREK
george clair	Henry CZERNY	maria conrad	Donna MITCHELL
mrs. gadd	Maia DANZIGER	helen wentworth	Barbara NEAL
pharmacist	Michael EGERMAN	claudia white	Nancy OPEL
marie earle	Christine FARRELL	dave gorman	Larry PINE
neil conrad	Glenn FITZGERALD	wendy hood	Christina RICCI
train conductor	Tom FLAGG	mikey's teacher	Marcell ROSENBLATT
ted franklin	Jonathan FREEMAN	pharmacy attendant	Wendy SCOTT
weather reporter	Barbara GARRICK	jim carver	Jamey SHERIDAN
stephen earle	Dennis GAZOMIROS	woman in pharmacy	Evelyn SOLANN
sandy carver	Adam HANN-BYRD	marge	Jessica STONE
mark boland	John Benjamin HICKEY	beth	Sarah THOMPSON
libbets casey	Katie HOLMES	janey carver	Sigourney WEAVER
dot halford	Allison JANNEY	paul's teacher	Scott WENTWORTH
pierce sawyer	Byron JENNINGS	rob halford	Rob WESTENBERG
sari steele	Colette KILROY	mikey carver	Elijah WOOD
ben hood	Kevin KLINE		
jack moellering	Ivan KRONENFELD		

stunt coordinators	G.A. Aguilar
	Douglas Crosby

stunts . . . . Jill Brown
Danny Downey
Lizzie Olesker
Susan Trout

unit production manager . . . . Alysse Bezahler
1st assistant directors . . . . Stephen Wertimer
James W. Murray, Jr.

2nd assistant directors . . . . Lisa Rowe
Brian O'Kelley

post production supervisors . . . Anthony Bregman
Kelly Miller

supervising sound editor . . . . Philip Stockton

re-recording mixer . . . . Reilly Steele
SOUND ONE

1st assistant editor . . . . Susan Littenberg

production supervisor . . . . Nancy Kriegel

2nd 2nd assistant director . . . . Linda Perkins

art director . . . . Bob Shaw
assistant art directors . . . . James Feng
Paul Kelly
Nicholas Lundy

art department coordinator . . . . Paige Bailey
set decorator . . . . Stephanie Carroll
assistant set decorator . . . . Jennifer Alex
storyboards . . . . Brick Mason
researcher . . . . Jean–Christophe Castelli

leadman . . . . Peter Dunbar
key set dresser . . . . Kelly Canfield

product placement & clearances . . . Wendy Cohen
asst. to production designer . . . . Tina Khayat
art department assistants . . . . Alisa Grifo
Robin Thomas
Mary Wigmore

set dressers . . . . Billy Bishop
Debbie Canfield
Scott Canfield
Charlie Foster
John Harajovic
Etienne Martine
Michael Murphy

Patrick Murphy
Peter Nauyokas
Mario Presterone
Paul Richards
Barret Schumacher
Paul Wilson
Kelly Winn

on-set dressers . . . . Jim Lillis
Travis Wright
charge scenic . . . . Elizabeth Linn

scenic forepersons . . . . Katy Dilkes
James Hoff

camera scenic . . . . Robert Barnett
key scenic shop person . . . . Emily Gaunt
scenic shop persons . . . . Tom Noucias
Chris Ruzek
shop production assistants . . . . Rob Landoll
Jesse Peliken

scenic artists . . . . Eric Bart
Steve Barth
Steve Caldwell
Marshall Carbee
Lauren Doner
Judy Evans
Michael Greene
Christopher Hébel
Richard Jones
Eugene Kagansky
Arcady Kotler
E. Reynold Maher
Vietta Maher
Michael Miles
Don Nance
John Paul
Cheryl Stewart

construction coordinator . . . . . Thomas Costabile
construction foreman . . . . Mark Mann
key carpenter . . . . Christopher J. Noonan

carpenters . . . . Judson Bell
Jack Coyle
Robert Dillon
John Farrell
Ed Gangloff
Claude Horstman
John McHugh
Genarro Proscia
Thomas White

key construction grip . . . . Robert W. Schmitt	electricians . . . . Michael Gallart
construction grip best boy . . . . Billy Van	Jamie Gallagher
construction grips . . . . James Brown	Timothy Healy
Joe Casillo	additional electricians . . . . Joseph R. Bruck
John Farina	Peter C. Caldwell
Ashalon Jones	Andy Niceberg
Monique Mitchell	Paul Steinberg
Vincent Reilly	day generator operator . . . . Daniel Canton
Frank Vigilante	
	rigging gaffers . . . . John Cardoni
camera operators . . . . Phil Oetiker	Peter Walts
John Sosenko	best boy rigging electric . . . . . Donald W. Schreck
	rigging electrics . . . . Bob Blair
1st assistant camera . . . . Andy Harris	Kobkeo Phothivongsa
2nd assistant camera . . . . Adam Gilmore	Perry Wolberger
camera loader . . . . Patrick Quinn	Chris Zizzo
video assist . . . . Ed Gleason	
24 frame playback . . . . Dennis Green	shop electrics . . . . David Levine
	Myron Odegaard
2nd unit photography . . . . Frank Prinzi	Brandon Odegaard
steadicam operators . . . . Andy Casey	key grip . . . . Jimmy Finnerty
Rick Rafael	best boy grip . . . . Tom Kerwick
	dolly grip . . . . Brad Goss
still photographers . . . . Adger Cowans	company grips . . . . Tony Campenni
Barry Wetcher	Joe Donahue
	Bill Jones
sound mixer . . . . Drew Kunin	Dave La Rue
	Bill Weberg
boom person . . . . Mark Goodermote	additional grip . . . . Steven E. Lawler
utility person . . . . Jeanne Gilliland	
	key rigging grip . . . . Jim McMillan, Jr.
property master . . . . Mark Peltzer	rigging grips . . . . Jim McMillan, Sr.
assistant property master . . . . Wally Adee	Tim McMillan
additional props . . . . Jonathan Tessler	
picture car production asst. . . . . Jacquie Hurd	make-up artists . . . . Michal Bigger
	James Sarzotti
stage manager . . . . Eric Zoback	assistant make-up . . . . Katie Bihr
assistant stage manager . . . . Virginia Plath	Frances Kohler
	ms. weaver's make-up . . . . Linda DeVetta
lead greensperson . . . . Will Scheck	
greens foreperson . . . . Graydon Pihlaja	hair stylist . . . . Aaron F. Quarles
greenspersons . . . . Pedro Barquin	assistant hair . . . . Donna Spahn
Guido DeCurtis	
Sean Lynch	associate costume designer . . . . Elizabeth Shelton
Darius Menard	wardrobe supervisors . . . Melissa Adzima-Stanton
Dominick Toto	Tom Stokes
standby greensperson . . . John "Butch" McCarthy	asst. to costume designer . . . . Leslie Yarmo
	wardrobe production asst. . . . . Anastasia Leopold
script supervisor . . . . Mary Cybulski	seamstress . . . . Laurie J. Buehler
gaffer . . . . Jonathan Lumley	wardrobe intern . . . . Frank Alberino
best boy electric . . . . Gary Hildebrand	location supervisor . . . . Declan Baldwin for
	FEATURELINE INC.

assistant location managers . . . . David Martin	unit publicists . . . . Jeff Hill, Millys Lee
Mike S. Ryan	CLEIN + WHITE
location coordinator . . . . Shannon Bowen	
location scouts . . . . David Graham	transportation captain . . . . Jimmy Nugent
Greg McHale	drivers . . . . Bob Anderson
location production assts. . . . . Laura Franses	
Janet Henry	
Ashley Sieg	

Frank Appedu	Paul Kane
Ed Blacknick	Joe Mallon
John Brady	Bobby Martini
Ted Brown, Jr.	George Moran
Jack Buckman	Robert Morgan
Jim Cablusky	Regis J. Mullaney
Steve Chartrand	Kevin O'Neil
Matt Calley	Danny Poseidento
Mike Canosa	Bob Rohr
James H. Chlebowski	Frank Scarvy
Tom Colovito	Kevin Smith
Richard Euell	Mike Stowe
Bobby Featherstone	Ray Sullivan
Al Gardner	Dan Thelen
Dan Haughton	John Uberti
Tony Ingrassellino	James Williams
Lenny Luizzi	Frank Young

production coordinator . . . . Beth A. Boyd
asst. production coordinator . . . . Libby Richman
production secretary . . . . Ryan Allen
office production assistants . . . . Chris Elam
Dean Haspiel
Stuart Nicolai
Matt Whitcher
production intern . . . . Bryan O'Cain
nyc office liaison . . . . Deidre Schrowang

asst. production manager . . . . John Rath
assistant unit manager . . . . Melissa Marr
set production assistants . . . . Jennifer M. Blais
John Craig
Apoovra Lakhia
Deanna Leslie
Alison Russo
Gregory John Smith
set intern . . . . Tracy Moore
film runner . . . . Paul Fischer

special effects supervisor . . . . John Ottesen

special effects . . . . Edward Drohan III
Edward Drohan IV
George Drohan
Greg Hagler
Daniel Ottesen
Ronald R. Ottesen, Jr.
Rich Pashayan
John Rapp
Ted Suchecki

assistant to mr. hope . . . . Hetakaisa Paarte
assistants to mr. lee . . . . Susanna Horng
David Lee
assistants to mr. schamus . . . . Sig Libowitz
Santiago Navila
Jessica Weigmann
auditor . . . . Craig Cannold
assistant auditor . . . . Olimpia T. Rinaldi
payroll accountant . . . Theresa Giardino Finnerty
accounting assistant . . . . Christine Hoppe
casting associate . . . . Julie Lichter
extras casting . . . . Judie Fixler
extras casting coordinator . . . . . Alyson Silverberg

parking coordinator . . . . Jose Tejada

tutors . . . . Rhona Gordon
Karin Nystrom
ON LOCATION TUTORS

craft service . . . . Gillian Malone
Martina Pozzi
caterers . . . . COAST TO COAST CATERING
MAINE COURSE CATERING

2nd assistant editors . . . . Ian Silverstein
Yasmine Amitai

sound effects designer . . . . Eugene Gearty
dialogue editor . . . . Fred Rosenberg
ADR Editor . . . . Marissa Littlefield

foley supervisor . . . . Bruce Pross
foley artist . . . . Marko Costanzo
foley editors . . . . Frank Kern
Kam Chan
assistant sound editors . . . . Julie Lindner
Chris Fielder
Benjamin Cheah
Todd Milner
Glenfield Payne

apprentice sound editor . . . . Gasuza Lwanga
sound effects intern . . . . Alan Zaleski

post production sound . . . . C5 INC.
sound coordinator . . . . Ghretta Hynd

ADR recordists . . David Boulton SOUND ONE
Andy Kris SPIN CYCLE POST, INC.

music editor . . . . Pat Mullins
asst. to music supervisor . . . . . . Maisie Weissman

projectionist . . . . Edmund Nardone

titles by . . . . BUREAU, N.Y.

digital visual effects by . . . . BALSMEYER &
EVERETT, INC.
supervisor . . . . Randy Balsmeyer
producer . . . . Kathy Kelehan
compositing supervisor . . . . Daniel Leung

train miniatures by . . SESSUMS ENGINEERING
Jack Sessums
Gary Maxwell
Michael Sajbel

post production accountant . . . . Joyce Hsieh
post production assistants . . . . Glen Basner
Ross Katz

negative cutters . . . . Stan & Patricia Sztaba
technicolor color timer . . . . Gloria Kaiser

dolby stereo consultant . . . . Tim J.Carroll

gamelan music by the EVERGREEN CLUB
GAMELAN ENSEMBLE
Bill Brennan
Mark Duggan
Paul Houle
Blair MacKay

north american native flutes . . . Daniel Cecil Hill
conductor . . . . Christopher Dedrick
orchestration . . . . Jamie Hopkings

score recorded and mixed by
Brad Haehnel at MANTA EASTERN SOUND,
Toronto

DIRTY LOVE
Written by Frank Zappa
Used by Permission of Munchkin Music
Performed by Frank Zappa
Courtesy of Rykodisc

SAMBA TRISTE
Written by Baden Powell & Billy Blanco
Used by Permission of Fermata do Brasil Ltda.
Performed by Stan Getz & Charlie Byrd
Courtesy of Verve Records
By Arrangement with
PolyGram Film & TV Licensing

TWO-PART INVENTION
IN B-FLAT MAJOR
Written by Johann Sebastian Bach
Performed by Wendy Carlos
Courtesy of Sony Classical
By Arrangement with Sony Music Licensing

SUAVECITO
Written by Richard Bean,
Abel Zarate & Pablo Tellez
Used by Permission of Canterbury Music
Performed by Malo
Courtesy of Warner Bros. Records Inc.
By Arrangement with Warner Special Products

SUGAR SUGAR
Written by Andy Kim & Jeff Barry
Used by Permission of EMI
Blackwood Music Inc. (BMI)
Performed by Wilson Pickett
Courtesy of Atlantic Recording Corp.
By Arrangement with Warner Special Products

THE MORNING AFTER
Written by Al Kasha & Joel Hirschhorn
Published by WB Music Corp. (ASCAP)/
Warner-Tamerlane Publishing Corp. (BMI)

I GOT A NAME
Written by Norman Gimbel & Charles Fox
Published by Warner-Tamerlane
Publishing Corp. (BMI)
Performed by Jim Croce
Courtesy of Saja Music Co.

TOO LATE TO TURN BACK NOW
Written by Eddie Cornelius
Used by Permission of EMI
Unart Catalog Inc. (BMI)
Performed by Cornelius Brothers & Sister Rose
Courtesy of EMI Records
Under License from EMI–Capitol
Music Special Markets

MONTEGO BAY
Written by Jeff Barry & Bobby Bloom
Used by Permission of EMI
Unart Catalog Inc. (BMI)
Performed by Bobby Bloom
Courtesy of Polydor Records
By Arrangement with
PolyGram Film & TV Licensing

O GRANDE AMOR
Written by Antonio Carlos Jobin
& Vinicius De Moraes
Used by Permission of Ipanema Music Corp.
Performed by Antonio Carlos Jobim
Courtesy of Verve Records
By Arrangement with
PolyGram Film & TV Licensing

COCONUT
Written by Harry Nilsson
Used by Permission of EMI
Blackwood Music Inc. (BMI)
Performed by Harry Nilsson
Courtesy of the RCA Records
Label of BMG Entertainment

LIGHT UP OR LEAVE ME ALONE
Written by Jim Capaldi
Used by Permission of Island Music Ltd.
Performed by Traffic
Courtesy of Island Records Limited
By Arrangement with
PolyGram Film & TV Licensing

HELP ME MAKE IT THROUGH THE NIGHT
Written by Kris Kristofferson
Used by Permission of Combine Music Corp.
Administered by EMI Blackwood Music Inc. (BMI)
Performed by Sammi Smith
Courtesy of Dominion Entertainment, Inc.

MR. BIG
Written by Andy Fraser, Simon Kirke,
Paul Kossof & Paul Rogers
Used by Permission of Blue Mountain Music, Ltd.
Performed by Free
Courtesy of A&M Records, Inc./
Island Records Limited
By Arrangement with
PolyGram Film & TV Licensing

COMPARED TO WHAT
Written by Gene McDaniels
Used by Permission of Lonport Music Corp.
Performed by Les McCann & Eddie Harris
Courtesy of Atlantic Recording Corp.
By Arrangement with Warner Special Products

LEVON
Written by Elton John & Bernie Taupin
Used by Permission of Dick James Music Ltd.
Performed by Elton John
Courtesy of Mercury Records Limited
By Arrangement with
PolyGram Film & TV Licensing

NIGHT LIGHTS
Written by Gerry Mulligan
Used by Permission of
Mulligan Publishing Co., Inc.
Performed by Gerry Mulligan
Courtesy of Verve Records
By Arrangement with
PolyGram Film & TV Licensing

I CAN'T READ
Written by David Bowie & Reeves Gabrels
Used by Permission of
Jones Music America (ASCAP)
Administered by RZO Music
Performed by David Bowie
Courtesy of Jones Music

Soundtrack from The Track Factory

President Nixon's News
Conference at San Clemente,
August 22, 1973. Courtesy of the
NIXON PRESIDENTIAL MATERIALS Staff
and the NATIONAL ARCHIVES

Divorce Court Courtesy of
RHODES PRODUCTIONS, Jack Rhodes, Sr.

Green Hornet Courtesy of
George W. Trendle, Jr., and
TWENTIETH CENTURY FOX TELEVISION

Ruffles Courtesy of
DAVIE-BROWN ENTERTAINMENT
on behalf of FRITO-LAY INC.

Vanishing Minds Courtesy of
THE COLLEGE FUND,
UNITED NEGRO COLLEGE FUND

M★A★S★H Courtesy of
TWENTIETH CENTURY FOX TELEVISION

Room 222 Courtesy of
TWENTIETH CENTURY FOX TELEVISION

Keep America Beautiful Courtesy of KEEP
AMERICA BEAUTIFUL, INC.

Time Tunnel Courtesy of
TWENTIETH CENTURY FOX TELEVISION

Special Thanks
NEW YORK CITY MAYOR'S OFFICE OF FILM,
THEATER AND BROADCASTING
Towns of Greenwich and New Canaan, Connecticut
Gayle Carpenter, Superintendent Robert Pegues,
Administrative Officer Peter G. Murphy: TOWN OF
NEW CANAAN, CONNECTICUT
Lieutenant Stephen Seiter (OIC&C),
Lieutenant Eric Weiner: STATE OF NEW YORK,
DIVISION OF MILITARY AND NAVAL AFFAIRS
Dante Brown, Claude Cargill, Cecil K. Watkins:
HARLEM TENNIS CENTER and THE HARLEM
JUNIOR TENNIS PROGRAM,
NANCY KRICORIAN LITERARY GROUPING

Art Contributions
Fritzi Ahadi, Rico Fonseca, GEMINI-G.E.L.,
Los Angeles,CA, Ellsworth Kelly, KRAUSHAAR
GALLERIES, INC., Mon Levinson,
Roy Lichtenstein, Peter Max, Leroy Neiman,
Robert Rauschenberg, Jodi Scherer
CASTELLI GRAPHICS, VAGA - VISUAL
ARTISTS, Sherle Wagner

UPSTAIRS / DOWNTOWN ANTIQUES
GRACIOUS HOME

Selected Jewelry provided by Johnny Lu
Ms. Weaver's Jewelry provided by Stephen Dweck

CONVERSE, CPC INTERNATIONAL,
DRAKES CAKES, CULINAR, ELLIOTS
AMAZING BEVERAGES, HAMMERMILL PAPER,
KASHI CEREALS, KIEHLS SINCE 1851, M&M
MARS CO., NEUTROGENA,
PENDLETON WOOLEN MILLS, PEZ

payroll . . . . ENTERTAINMENT PARTNERS
insurance . . . . Ross Miller,
Amy Schultz DISC INSURANCE
projector equipment provided by . . BOSTON LIGHT
AND SOUND
opticals by . . . . THE EFFECTS HOUSE
post production editing services by . . . . GOOD EDIT,
INC
lenses and Arri ® cameras by . . . CAMERA SERVICE
CENTER
dailies by . . . . DUART FILM & VIDEO
color by . . . . TECHNICOLOR
prints by . . . . DELUXE

Copyright © 1997 by TWENTIETH CENTURY
FOX FILM CORPORATION. All Rights Reserved.

TWENTIETH CENTURY FILM CORPORATION
is the author of this motion picture for
purposes of copyright and other laws.

The events, characters, and firms depicted in this
photoplay are fictitious. Any similarity to
actual persons, living or dead, or to actual
events or firms is purely coincidental.

Ownership of this motion picture is protected by
copyright and other applicable law, and any
unauthorized duplication, distribution or
exhibition of this motion picture could result
in criminal prosecution as well as civil liability.

RELEASED BY TWENTIETH CENTURY FOX

ABOUT THE AUTHORS

ANG LEE was born in Taiwan in 1954 and moved to the U.S. in 1978 where he received his BFA in theater from the University of Illinois, and his MFA in film production from New York University. In 1983 he won the Taiwanese Golden Harvest Film Festival Best Narrative Film award for his film *Dim Lake*. While at NYU he made *Fine Line,* which received Best Director and Best Film at the 1985 NYU Film Festival.

Pushing Hands, Ang Lee's first feature screened in the Panorama section of the 1992 Berlin Film Festival, won Best Film in the Asian-Pacific Festival, was nominated for nine Golden Horse awards (the Taiwanese Academy Award) and won three, including a Special Jury Prize for Ang Lee's direction.

In 1994, *The Wedding Banquet* premiered at the Berlin Film Festival (1993) and was awarded Berlin's top prize, The Golden Bear. The film garnered tremendous critical praise and box office success. *Variety* heralded it as "the most profitable film in the world in 1993." The film was nominated for the Academy and Golden Globe Awards for Best Foreign Language Film and six Independent Spirit awards. In Taiwan, *The Wedding Banquet* received five Golden Horse awards, including awards for Best Film and Best Director.

Eat Drink Man Woman, the third film in Ang Lee's "Father Knows Best" trilogy, premiered as the opening night film in the Director's Fortnight at the Cannes Film Festival (1994) and was nominated for Academy and Golden Globe Awards. In addition, the film was voted Best Foreign Language Film by the National Board of Review.

In 1995, Ang Lee directed *Sense and Sensibility,* starring Emma Thompson, Hugh Grant, and Kate Winslet, with a screenplay by Thompson. The film was nominated for seven Academy Awards, including Best Picture, and won the Oscar for Best Screenplay Adaptation. In addition, the film received the Golden Bear Award at the Berlin Film Festival, as well as Golden Globes for Best Screenplay and Best Film. One of the most critically acclaimed films of the year, *Sense and Sensibility* was featured in over 100 Ten Best Films lists for 1995, and was lauded by the New York Film Critics (Best Director), the Boston Film Critics (Best Film, Best Director), and the National Board of Review (Best Film, Best Director).

In 1996, Ang Lee completed *The Ice Storm,* his first feature on an entirely American subject, which was adapted from the acclaimed novel by Rick Moody, and stars Kevin Kline, Sigourney Weaver, and Joan Allen.

JAMES SCHAMUS founded the film production company Good Machine with Ted Hope in 1991, the year he also began teaching in the film division of Columbia University's School of the Arts. In the six years since Good Machine's founding, Schamus and Hope have emerged as two of the most critically and commercially successful producers in the independent film world. Among Schamus's credits are the films that have resulted from his longstanding collaboration with the director Ang Lee: *Pushing Hands* (1991, Producer and Co-Writer); *The Wedding Banquet* (1992, Producer and Co-Writer); *Eat Drink Man Woman* (1993, Associate Producer and Co-Writer); *Sense and Sensibility* (1995, Co-Producer); and the forthcoming *The Ice Storm,* starring Kevin Kline and Sigourney Weaver (Producer and Writer). Among the other twenty films with which Schamus has been associated are four of the past six Sundance Film Festival Grand Prize winners: Edward Burns's *The Brothers McMullen* (1995, Executive Producer); Tom Noonan's *What Happened Was…* (1994, Executive Producer); Alexandre Rockwell's *In the Soup* (1992, Associate Producer); and Todd Haynes's *Poison* (1991, Executive Producer). Schamus also served as executive producer on Haynes's *Safe* (1995). At Columbia University, Schamus teaches a wide variety of courses, from the history of the film musical to an introduction to film theory. This screenplay for *The Ice Storm* was awarded Best Screenplay Prize at Cannes.